Bipolar Disorder General Aspects

Marcus Deminco

Translated by Ilka Andrade Suarez
Copyright © 2019 - Marcus Deminco
All Rights Reserved | Salvador – Bahia – Brazil
ISBN: 9781794675131
Independently published

Summary

Historical Aspects

The terms "mania" and "melancholy" date back to several centuries before Christ, and still correspond approximately to their original concepts. Although more comprehensive and imprecise, in their main aspects, they very much resemble the descriptions of what is now called bipolar disorder. Among the ancients, studies show that it was Arameteus from Cappadocia, who lived in Alexandria in the first century AD, who wrote the main texts that have reached the present day concerning the oneness of manic-depressive illness.

In chapter V of his book On the Etiology and Symptomatology of Chronic Diseases, Araeteus wrote: "I think that melancholia is the beginning and as such part of the mania ... The development of mania is the result of worsening melancholia, rather than being the shift to a different disease. "More explicitly, he wrote: "In most melancholics sorrow becomes better after various periods of time, and becomes joy, and patients develop what is called mania." (AKISKAL, 1996 apud DEL-PORTO, 2005)

In antiquity, Hippocrates already described melancholy (using it as a synonym for depression) and mania, but did not propose the union between the two pictures. According to him, the variations resulted from imbalance of the body fluids, the so-called moods, so they could have cyclical changes, associated with changes in emotional states. This theory has lasted until some cyclical mood descriptions emerged in the nineteenth century, suggesting that they would be distinct forms of the same disease. Also, in the mid-nineteenth century, not far removed from the modern concept of "manic-depressive insanity," French psychiatrist and neurologist Jules Baillarger described a new type of insanity, called "la folie à double forme", whose main characteristic was the occurrence of episodes of mania and depression in the same patient. (ANGST, 2001 apud ALCANTARA, 2003)

In the last century, the German psychiatrist Emil Kraepelin separated the Early Dementias (which would come to be called schizophrenia) from Manic-Depressive Psychoses (PMD). He argued that PMDs consisted of a set of diseases whose most prominent symptoms were mood swings. No distinction was made between people who manifested only depression and those who had only symptoms of mania.

All were classified and treated equally, as PMD patients. It was as if there were two poles: patients with pure depression and pure mania, and in the middle would be most of them, with varying portions of depression and mania. In the 8th edition of his book: "Psychiatrie: Ein Lehrbuch fur Studierende und Artze." Kraepelin (1910 apud DEL-PORTO, 2005) classified mixed states with great similarity as the current hips in their classification of mixed states. (TABLE 1)

TYPES	HUMOR	ACTIVITY	THOUGHT
Anxious or Depressive Mania	—	+	+
Agitated depression	—	+	—
Mania with Inhibition of Thought	+	+	—
Manic stupor	+	—	—
Depression with Idea Escape	—	—	+
Inhibited Mania	+	—	+

Table 1. Classification of mixed states.
(KRAEPELIN, 1910 apud Ibidem)

However, it was not until the 1950s that there was a tendency to separate those people who manifested pictures of mania and depression from those who only had depressive episodes; calling the first of bipolar and the last of unipolar. Studies have shown that patients with unipolar depression had more family members with depressive symptoms, while bipolar patients had more relatives with the same symptoms.

The unipolar mania was then integrated into the concept of "Bipolar Disorder". Subsequently, a subdivision also gained strength in distinguishing patients within this spectrum: type I bipolar (manias and depressions) and type II bipolar (hypomania and depressions). In addition to Bipolar Disorder Not Otherwise Specified (BSO): disorders with bipolar aspects that do not meet the criteria for any subtype of the specific TBs. (DSM-V apud LAMBERT, 2006).

The concept of unipolar "depression", also described as "major depression", became popular and facilitated the diagnosis of depression, which began to be made more and more by doctors of other specialties, other health professionals. Today, the term "bipolar spectrum" is gaining ground in scientific circles and is increasingly being broadcast in the media. The name resembles ghosts or nightmares, but also defines one of the main characteristics of the disorder: the variation of states. According to this concept, the bipolar spectrum refers to the range of clinical presentations of the disease, which can range from one pole to another, from pure unipolar depression to episodes of hypomania, depression to mania, to pure mania.

There are two denominations used for the disorder: Bipolar Affective Disorder and Bipolar Mood Disorder, the latter considered the most appropriate term currently. This difference of nomenclature is due to the concepts of affection and humor, which are technically different. In a simple way, the first refers to the emotions that arise quickly in the face of changing a specific situation - with the feeling of joy when you get a gift, sadness to know that it was wrong in a test, irritation when the opposing team makes a goal in a championship final or fear when some pain arises suddenly and one thinks about the possibility of being a victim of a serious illness.

Already moods refer to longer emotional states, which last for hours, days or weeks, and can influence the individual's way of thinking and acting. An example would be depressive mood. Among other manifestations, we can think of this picture as follows: for no apparent reason, the person wakes up several days in a row with dismay, as if sadness were the background of his life; the imprints on her own self become more negative and critical, or she believes her colleagues or relatives evaluate her in a negative, demeaning way.

The concept of "Bipolar Disorder" focuses on mood swings - one of its poles is depressive mood and another - the euphoric. However, it is not just humor that gets changed in Bipolar Disorder. Many other brain and extra-cerebral functions undergo changes, such as those related to biological rhythms, to the control of bodily movements (with the predominance of agitation or body slowness) of the functions of memory and mental concentration, impulsiveness and pleasure, both small things in life (taking care of the home, hobbies) and sexual desire. TB would be better understood as the disease of instabilities, and that of humor is more noticeable.

Definition and Prevalence

Bipolar Disorder (TB), also known as "Bipolar Affective Disorder" and originally called "Manic-Depressive Insanity," is a psychiatric condition characterized by severe mood swings involving periods of high mood and depression (affective experience) interspersed with periods of remission, and are associated with specific cognitive, physical and behavioral symptoms. (CLEMENT, 2015)

According to the new global report of the World Health Organization (WHO, 2016) the number of people with depression increased by 18% between 2005 and 2015. Within this context, Bipolar Disorder (TB) is a relatively frequent psychiatric condition, it is a chronic disease which affects between 1% and 2% of the population and represents one of the leading causes of disability in the world. It is estimated that about 4% of the adult world population suffers from Bipolar Disorder. The Brazilian Association of Bipolar Disorder (ABTB, 2016) confirms that this prevalence is also valid for Brazil, which represents about 6 million people in the country.

According to the 10th review of the International Statistical Classification of Diseases and Related Health Problems (ICD-10), Bipolar Affective Disorder is characterized by the presence of two or more episodes in which mood levels and patient activities are significantly disturbed. Oscillating between episodes of mood elevation and increased energy and activity (hypomania or mania), and periods of decreased mood and decreased energy and activity (depression). In general terms, ICD-10 also considers that Bipolar Affective Disorder (F31) should be classified according to the type of the current episode, in hypomanic, manic or depressive episodes. Manic episodes are subdivided according to the presence or absence of psychotic symptoms, while depressive episodes are classified as mild, moderate or severe. Mild and moderate episodes may be classified according to the presence or absence of somatic symptoms. Severe episodes are subdivided according to the presence or absence of psychotic symptoms.

However, for the 5th edition of the Diagnostic and Statistical Manual of Mental Disorders (DSM-V), the disorder differs in two main types: Type I, in which the mood elevation is severe and persists (mania); Type II, in which the elevation of mood is milder (hypomania). The use of the "mixed characteristics" specifier applies to states where there is a concomitant occurrence of manic and depressive symptoms, although these are seen as mood poles. The Cyclothymic Disorder is characterized by the alternation between hypomanic and depressive periods over at least two years in adults (or one year in children) without, however, meeting the criteria for an episode of mania, hypomania or major depression.

The DSM also includes the category "other Bipolar Disorder and related disorder specified" to classify atypical conditions, marked by the occurrence of symptoms that do not meet the minimum duration and frequency criteria to characterize even one episode of hypomania.

Estimates from the World Health Organization (WHO) indicate that TB affects approximately 30 million people worldwide and is among the biggest causes of disability. Data from a combined sample of eleven countries revealed that lifetime prevalence rates of Type I Bipolar Disorder (TB-I), Type II Bipolar Disorder (TB-II), Subsyndromal Bipolar Disorder (TB-sub) and bipolar spectrum (EB) were 0.6%, 0.4%, 1.4% and 2.4% respectively. The annual prevalence rates of TB-I, TB-II, TB-sub and EB fell to 0.4%, 0.3%, 0.8% and 1.5%, respectively.

In Brazil, more specifically in the city of São Paulo, the prevalence rate of TB (without differentiating subtypes) throughout life was 1% and the annual prevalence was 0.5%. The mortality rate is also high, and the most frequent reason for death among affected young people is suicide. About 25% of adolescents with TB have suicidal behaviors. Many patients also use alcohol and / or drugs, which aggravates the symptoms even more. (WALTERS, 2002 apud BOSAIPO, BORGES, JURUENA, 2016).

In type II bipolar patients, more than 95% of disease time corresponds to the depressive phase with a few characteristics of TB. With this unipolar / bipolar distinction, new studies were done and it was observed that for each bipolar patient, there are 20 unipolar depressives. But it soon became apparent that most bipolar patients initially had depressive episodes, which confused the diagnosis. And about 20% of the total of unipolar tended to evolve into bipolar conditions. The unipolar / bipolar classification became official both in the 10th edition of the International Statistical Classification of Diseases and Related Health Problems (ICD-10) and in the 5th edition of the Diagnostic and Statistical Manual of Mental Disorders (DSM-V).

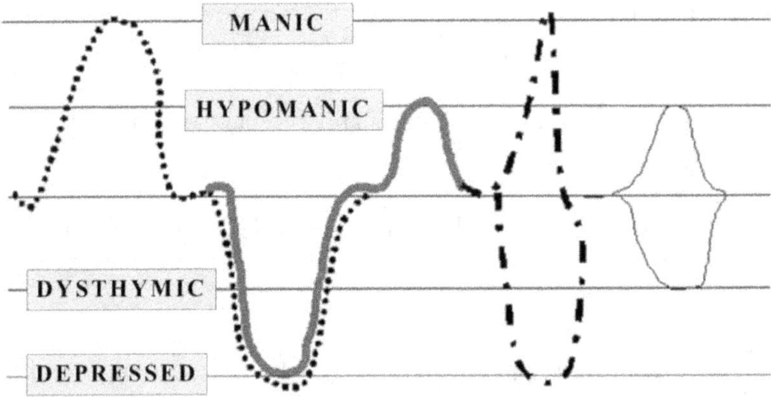

Figure 1. Graphical representation of mood disorders.
(STAHL, 2013 apud BOSAIPO, BORGES, JURUENA, 2016)

The Phases of Disorder

One very well described and systematized aspect of the disorder is the definition of mood seizures, phases or "episodes", when many symptoms arise, defining a specific picture. Recently, the characteristics that appear between the crises, such as irritable, hyperactive, depressive, impulsive temperaments and the daily consequences of being unstable, such as relationship difficulties, staying in a job or maintaining friendships have been studied and described. durable.

Although TB has four types of pathological episodes characterized as depressive, hypomanic, manic and mixed - it can be considered basically a depressive illness, since most patients spend much of their life at this pole of the disease. There are, however, lighter forms of manifestation of these episodes, in which the characteristics of the person are mixed, seeming to form a basic structure, a temperament that manifests itself in childhood or adolescence and is confused with the individual's "way of being."

Depressive Episode

In addition to the pathological connotation, the word "depression" generally brings to mind people's bad phases of life. In some contexts, the term is used broadly in analogy with periods of economic crisis. It has also become common to use the word as synonymous with sadness, despair, or anguish.

Depression is usually triggered by a significant loss such as death of a loved one, loss of employment, a disillusionment of love, or even a highly stressful life stage because of work or family problems. The fact is that, from a clinical point of view, depression affects the individual's way of thinking, acting, and being and should be seen as a health problem that affects not only the brain and the psychological state but also virtually every organism.

Sadness, a frequent feature of depression, is a universal experience. It is an emotion experienced in a negative, unpleasant way that, in order not to revive it, the individual avoids unpleasant situations in the future. In general terms, we may think that if a student scores a low grade in school, the sadness of going through this situation, associated with failure, would lead him to reevaluate his way of studying so that he would not receive bad grades again. According to such a theory, sadness triggers the introspective movement, people isolate themselves from the outside world "by recognizing themselves" to reflect on how the unpleasant situation happened and how it could be done so that it would not happen again. In this way, sadness would help in the process of maturation, preparing us to better face a life that is by its nature filled with inevitable losses and frustrations.

It can arise on a day to day basis as a result of something bad that has occurred, or when memories of past events provoke it. In general, in these cases, it is small in intensity and short in duration. The more insistent state, called a depressive mood, contaminates the perception of what is happening in that period. A common everyday situation such as seeing a child begging in a corner can be perceived more distressingly if the individual is in a depressed mood, whereas at another time this same situation would cause transient discomfort, indifference, or even rage.

Depressive mood, usually associated with a loss, is often linked to physical discomfort, such as a cold or premenstrual phase. It can often come with physical sensations such as restlessness, anxiety, crying, feeling distressing pressure or weight in the chest. But to what extent can this feeling be considered normal, and when does it become pathological, that is, a symptom of depression?

Although it is not a very precise criterion, it is possible to take into account its duration time. Sadness becomes worrying, for example, if it predominates over much of the patient's day, or if it occurs on most days. Its intensity is a very precise criterion, since each has its own "measure" to evaluate it, and what is intense for one would be almost imperceptible for another. In addition, it can vary according to the time of day, and can thus distort the perception of intensity.

A person who gets bad news can feel a deep anguish that lasts a few minutes, and remember to have had a very sad day. Another, who feels moderate sadness every day, almost all the time, can consider this normal day, the same as the previous day or last week, when he was sad too. But when it happens that the person is crying, often for reasons that seem not justified, or when he feels anguish, in an intensity difficult to be tolerated, something that clearly affects his daily life, this sadness can be considered excessive. In general, people find it more difficult to differentiate the so-called normal sadness from its pathological manifestation (typical of depression) when it arises after a justifiable event, such as the loss of a loved one, which could fully justify a more intense and lasting sadness.

Although this type of situation in most people, after a few weeks or months (depending on the case), the tendency is for the individual to resume his activities, despite the pain of loss and longing. When this sadness continues, and especially if sadness interferes with the individual's life, it is probably a pathological symptom. Often, the person suffering from pathological sadness has difficulty admitting that he is ill and justifies his condition with arguments such as unemployment, loneliness, financial difficulties or incomprehension of important people in his life. What this person rarely realizes is that others undergo similar circumstances and may react in other ways and that several of these situations may be consequence and not cause of melancholy.

Patients often allude to the feeling that everything seems futile, or unimportant. They believe they have lost the ability to feel joy or pleasure in life. Everything seems to them empty and bland, the world is seen "without colors", without shades of joy. In children and adolescents, above all, humor can be irritable, or "grumpy", rather than sad. Some patients appear to be "apathetic" rather than sad, often referring to "feelings of lack of feeling." They find, for example, that they are no longer moved by the arrival of the grandchildren, or by the suffering of a loved one, and so on.

The depressed person often feels a burden to family and friends, often invoking death to relieve those who watch him in illness. Suicide ideas are frequent and fearsome. The motivations for suicide include cognitive distortions (perceiving any difficulties as definite and insurmountable obstacles, tending to overestimate the losses suffered), and the intense desire to put an end to an extremely painful and endless emotional state. Still others seek death as a way to atone for their supposed faults. Thoughts of suicide range from the remote desire to be simply dead, to minute plans to kill yourself (establishing the mode, time, and place for the act). Thoughts about death should be systematically investigated, since such conduct may prevent suicidal acts, giving the patient the opportunity to express himself or herself about it. (WIDLÖCHER, 1983 apud DEL PORTO, 1999)

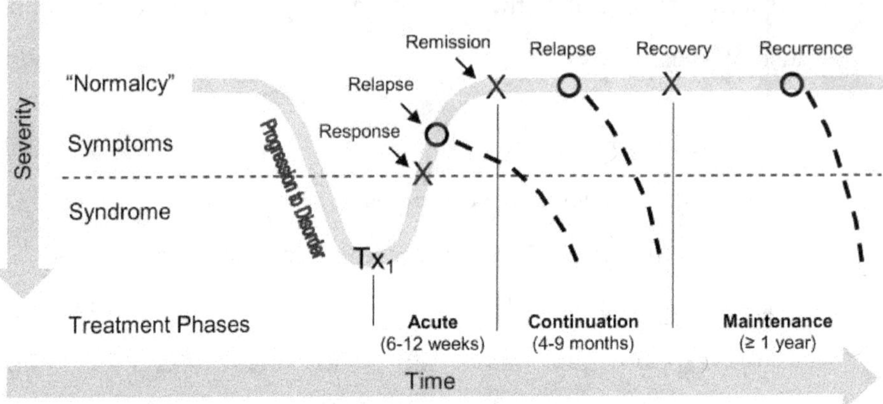

Figure 2. Phases of treatment during the depressive episode.
(KUPFER, 1991, apud FLECK, 2009)

Manic Episode

The DSM defines Mania as the presence for at least one week of irritable, expansive or elevated mood associated with three or more of the following symptoms, with severity sufficient to cause functional impairment (work problems, relationships, need for hospitalization, psychotic symptoms) : increased self-esteem / grandiosity, decreased need for sleep, being more talkative / pressured to talk, fast thinking / brain drain, distraction, psychomotor agitation / increased activity, excessive involvement with pleasurable activities that can have disastrous consequences. Hypomania, in turn, is defined by the presence of persistently irritable, expansive, or elevated mood over at least four days associated, or at least three of those same symptoms reported for mania, but with less severity, without significant functional impairment.

The term "mania" is often understood by lay people as unusual and repetitive behavior. Already "manic" describes that individual who has behaviors extremely deviated from the accepted norm, usually associated with perversions. For health professionals, however, the term "mania" represents the euphoric pole of mood disorder. The curious thing is that, although the excessive euphoria is very characteristic and evident in these pictures, he is not always present in a manic episode.

The most common symptoms are irritability (which can lead to occasional aggression) and hyperactivity. Other symptoms of mania include decreased sleepiness, sudden high self-esteem, excessive speech, difficulty focusing attention, and involvement with pleasurable but dangerous activities such as excessive spending and shopping, impulsive acts, drug use, indiscretions, and increased sexual activity.

The patient in mania does not notice his own alteration, he has the impression of being extremely well, as if he lived the best phase of his life. For him, it is the others who have problems. In some cases, the person in this state, with aggression and impulsiveness exacerbated, needs to be protected of itself, since at this stage of the disorder can commit acts that will regret in the future, certain situations. It is common that, after the end of a crisis of mania, the patient is ashamed of his attitudes.

Euphoria can be defined as excessive and exaggerated joy, which remains independent of external events. The person in this state shows exaggerated optimism and relates to people very easily, especially when it comes to strangers. In the most serious forms, he even believes he can be famous. It is common for sudden mood swings to occur: when you remember, for example, your mother's death, you burst into tears, and after a few minutes you continue to laugh.

The person tries to do many things at the same time, has difficulty staying still, can not concentrate on a single activity and distracts easily. Some even exhibit auditory or visual illusions and manifest paranoid behavior. These symptoms can be confused with schizophrenia, especially if they occur at the onset of the disease. Anxiety, panic attacks (with pronounced physical discomfort: sweating, tachy-cardia, shortness of breath, dizziness, etc.) or obsessive symptoms are also likely to occur. Not all these manifestations appear in a crisis of mania, but can make difficult the diagnosis.

Technically, hypomania is a phase of mania lighter, with the same symptoms, but less intense and evident. In practice, it can be considered "invisible", as it usually goes unnoticed and can be inter-preted as a phase of greater productivity in work, creativity and so-cialization. But there is one relevant fact: Hypomania is an indicator that the person suffers from Bipolar Disorder. In general, the mania starts abruptly and lasts from a few days to a few weeks.

Manic episodes are often shorter than depressive episodes. Un-fortunately, manic episodes are often followed by depressive episodes putting the patient on an emotional "roller coaster." Although some patients report that the euphoria they experience when they are man-ic can be rewarding and enjoyable, these episodes usually occur at large personal costs. They affect marriages, business, finances and patients' health and lead to exhaustion, the occasional use of sub-stances and other risky behaviors that put the patient in frequent danger. In the extreme, the manic individual has a higher risk of dy-ing from cardiac complications and a greater tendency to commit suicide in the transition from mania to depression when they under-stand how inappropriate their behavior was. (ANDREASEN and BLACK, 2009)

Mixed Episode

The symptoms of Bipolar Disorder do not always appear in block, like typical of depression or mania / hypomania. Manic behaviors may appear in the middle of a depressive episode - vice versa. When there is such a mixture, recognition and treatment are confusing, with depressive moods in which the agitation is striking, which may worsen with the use of antidepressants, and depressed moods that are mistaken for depression. It is a potentially serious form of the disorder, because when there is a mixture of agitation and thoughts of death tempered with great impulsiveness, the risk of suicide is enormous. During an episode or mixed state, symptoms often include restlessness, disturbed sleep, major changes in appetite, and suicidal thoughts. People in a mixed state may feel very sad or hopeless and at the same time extremely energized.

A Mixed Episode is characterized by a period of time (at least 1 week) during which the criteria for both Manic Episode and Major Depressive Episode are met almost every day. The individual experiences a rapid alternation of mood (sadness, irritability, euphoria), accompanied by the symptoms of a Manic Episode and a Major Depressive Episode. Symptomatic presentation often involves restlessness, insomnia, appetite dysregulation, psychotic features, and suicidal thinking. The disturbance must be severe enough to cause severe impairment in social or occupational functioning or to require hospitalization, or is marked by the presence of psychotic features. The disturbance is not due to the direct physiological effects of a substance (eg, drug of abuse, medication or other treatment) or a general medical condition (eg, hyperthyroidism). Symptoms such as those seen in a Mixed Episode may be due to the direct effects of antidepressant medications, electroconvulsive therapy, phototherapy, or prescription drugs for other general medical conditions (eg, corticosteroids).

If a person with recurrent Major Depressive Disorder, for example, develops a mixed symptom during antidepressant drug treatment, the diagnosis of the episode is Substance-Induced Mood Disorder with Mixed Characteristics, and there is no change in the diagnosis of Major Depressive Disorder for Bipolar I Disorder. Some evidence suggests the possible existence of a bipolar "diathesis" in individuals who develop mixed-type episodes after somatic treatment for depression. These individuals may be more likely to have future non-substance Manic, Mixed or Hypomanic Episodes or somatic treatments for depression. This consideration may be especially important in the case of children and adolescents.

Mixed Episodes may evolve from a Manic Episode or Major Depressive Episode or may emerge as something new. For example, the diagnosis can be changed from Bipolar I, Most Recent Manic Episode, to Bipolar I, Most Recent Mixed Episode, in the case of an individual with 3 weeks of manic symptoms followed by a week of both manic and depressive symptoms. Mixed Episodes can last from weeks to months, presenting remission to a period with few or no symptoms or progressing to a Major Depressive Episode. More rarely, a Mixed Episode evolves into a Manic Episode. (BALDAÇARA, 2015)

Therefore, the combination of changes in these domains made up the clinical picture of the disease. In the pure states of mania or depression, the three domains are altered in the same direction. In typical mania, for example, there would be exaltation of humor, flight of ideas and increased motor activity; in typical depression there would be sad mood, thought inhibition, and psychomotor slowness. Differently, in mixed states these domains were modified in different directions, that is, there would be a mixture of elements of manic and melancholy in the fields of humor, the course of thought, and psychomotricity. Among the mixed states, six types were distinguished: depressive (or anxious or furious) mania, unproductive mania (or impaired thinking), inhibited mania (with motor inhibition), manic stupor, depression with brain drain, and agitated depression. (DOYLE, 1998 apud CLEMENTE, 2015)

There are, however, controversies about the relationship between mixed states and bipolar rapid cycling disorders. It is doubtful whether such phenomena correspond to the same process, characterized by the rapid alternation of mood, that is, the mixed state, in fact correspond to an extremely rapid cycling frame; however, the most accepted hypothesis is that they constitute distinct phenomena. Thus, we consider the existence of unstable mixed states, the rapid alternation of opposing affective states, and therefore associated with the speed of cycling, which would be different from stable mixed states, in which the symptoms of mania and depression are simultaneously present. (SCHWARTZMANN, 2004, apud CLEMENTE, 2015)

25

The Neurobiological Bases of TB

There are multiple etiological factors in mood disorders, resulting from the combination of individual (personality, personal and personal) environmental factors (diet, alcohol, rhythms) that trigger the disease in biologically vulnerable individuals. Both depression and mania are thought to be the result of various psychological, environmental, genetic and biological processes. (AKISKAL, 2000 apud NETO and ELKIS, 2009)

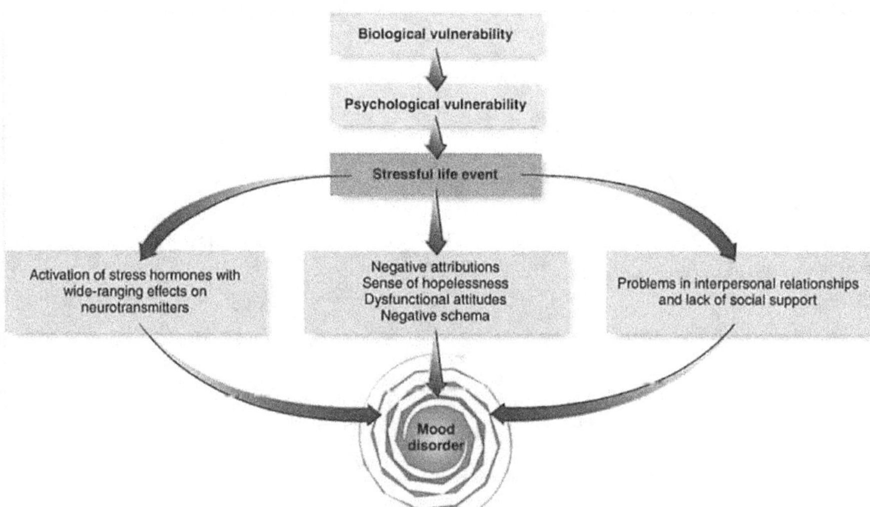

Figure 3. Integrated Model of Mood Disorders. (BARLOW, 2008)

Changes in functional evidence, neurochemical and behavioral integration models that have been observed in the processes of pleasure, reward and disturbance of circadian rhythms in patients with Affective Disorder. The Limbic System represents the region of convergence of these factors, producing imbalance of biogenic amines, specifically Noradrenaline, Serotonin and, in the background, Dopamine, and secondary messenger systems (eg, Adenyl Cyclase) and Neuroactive Peptides. In addition, dysregulation of the endocrine, hypothalamic-adrenal, thyroid and growth hormone-linked dyads, sleep abnormalities, circadian rhythm disorders, abnormalities of the immune system and cerebral morphophysiological changes occur.

In the genesis of mood disorders, genetic factors are fundamental, especially in Bipolar Disorder. About 50% of type I bipolar disorder have at least one parent with Affective Disorder, especially depression; if one of the parents is carrying TB I, the chance of one of the children having mood disorders is 25%, which rises to 50% to 75% in case both parents are affected. Psychosocial factors in general represent triggers of mood disorders, for example, job loss, loved ones, separations. There are no personality traits predisposing to mood disorder, depression can occur in any type of personality. (NETO and ELKIS, 2009)

The literature review by Baumann and Bogerts (2001) suggests that the brains of patients suffering from Bipolar Disorder differ significantly from those who are not suffering from mood disorders. Specifically, basal ganglia are somewhat smaller in bipolar and depressive patients. The most drastic reductions are found in the Accumbens Nucleus, the fundamental structure in translating environmental stimuli to the motivation to respond. Structural deficits are also found in the dorsal nucleus of Rafe, the site of Serotonin production.

In another literary review, through neuroimaging studies, abnormalities were found in the striatum, the amygdala and the prefrontal cortex. This review supports the notion of the involvement of frontal-subcortitial circuits in Bipolar Disorder. In addition, a reduction in cerebellar size was detected. The most common result in studies with MRI is the presence of white matter hyperintensities at rates higher than expected. The hyperintensities of the white matter are small areas characterized by a signal of greater intensity than the surrounding tissue. These hyperintensities are more commonly found in the elderly and in individuals who have suffered cardiovascular events. In addition, processes such as demyelination, astrogliosis (formation of new astrocytes or growth of existing astrocytes) or axonal loss may lead to the formation of hyperintensities of the white matter. (YURGELUN-TODD et al., 2000 apud Ibidem)

Although these abnormalities are seen in bipolar patients at higher than expected rates, the finding that most bipolar individuals do not present hyperintensities suggests that they may play a minimal causative role in the disorder. Thus, they are more likely to form because of the lifestyle characteristic of patients with manias (high rates of substance abuse and cardiovascular risk) than by the subject's susceptibility to Bipolar Disorder. There was less overall glucose metabolic activity in the brains of patients with bipolar depression than in those with bipolar mania. Although one study identified increased cerebral blood flow during episodes of mania, most studies did not observe differences in blood flow in bipolar mania or depression, compared to healthy control subjects (STRAKOWSKI et al., 2000 apud Ibidem)

Studies of Susceptibility Genes (genes that increase susceptibility to disease) have already implicated the chromosomes: 4, 12, 18 and 21, among others. Currently one of the most powerful links found is in the region 12q23-q24.40. Results of genome screening suggest the existence of several susceptibility loci in the chromosomes: 1, 6, 7, 10, 16 and 22. Another recent study suggests loci in regions: 13q32 and 1q32.32. (GINNS, 1998 apud ALDA, 1999)

A polymorphism in the promoter region with two allelic variants, a long and a short insertion / deletion of 44 base pairs, is studied. Possible functional role of this polymorphism in which the short allele would recapture less serotonin than the long allele. (DU E COLL, 1999 apud VIEIRA, 2006) Studies in the cerebrospinal fluid and urinary levels of TB patients compared with Normal Control Groups found an imbalance in the regulation of Biogenic Amines (distributed in the Limbic System), demonstrating changes in the systems:

1) Noradrenergic;

2) Serotonergic;

3) Dopaminergic;

4) Cholinergic.

Symptom Dimension	Implicated Regions In Bipolar	Implicated Regions In Schizophrenia
Disorganization	• Hypofunction in the ventrolateral prefrontal cortex (vlPFC) • Hypofunction in the medial prefrontal cortex(mPFC)/ACC	• Hypofunction in the medial prefrontal cortex(mPFC) • Hypofunction in the dorsolateral prefrontal cortex(dlPFC) • Hypofunction in the cerebellum • Hypofunction in the insula • Hypofunction in the temporal cortex
Reality Distortion	• Functional abnormalities in prefrontal and thalamic regions	• Reduced grey matter in perisylvian and thalamic regions • Hypofunction of the amygdala, mPFC, and hippocampus/parahippocampus
Psychomotor Povery	• Functional abnormalities in the vlPFC and ventral striatum	• Reduced grey matter in the vlPFC, mPFC and dlPFC • Reduced grey matter in the striatum, thalamus, amygdala and temporal cortices

Table 2. Specific symptoms have been linked to various neuroimaging abnormalities in bipolar disorder, as well as schizophrenia. Reality distortion, disorganization, and psychomotor poverty have been linked to prefrontal, thalamic, and striatal regions in both schizophrenia and bipolar. (FRANGOU, 2014)

Studies examining resting blood flow, or metabolism generally observed abnormalities dependent upon mood state. Bipolar depression is generally associated with dlPFC and mOFC hypometabolism. Less consistent associations include reduced temporal cortex metabolism, increased limbic metabolism and reduced ACC metabolism. Mania is also associated with dlPFC and OFC hypometabolism. Limbic hypermetabolism is more consistent than in bipolar depression, but the overall study quality is low due to limitations associated with neuroimaging in acutely manic patients. Another review reported that mania is generally associated with frontal/ventral hypoactivation, while depression is generally associated with the opposite. A degree of lateralization with regard to abnormalities has been reported, with mania being associated with the right hemisphere, and depression the left. Trait abnormalities in euthymic patients have been observed, including hypoactivity in the ventral prefrontal cortex, and hyper-actvity in the amygdala. (CHEN et al., 2011)

Diagnosis

A person with Bipolar Disorder (TB) is diagnosed, usually only ten years after the first attempts at treatment. Before that, the patient may be informed that he suffers from the most varied problems, such as drug addiction, obesity, personality and character disorder, panic disorder etc., however, the misdiagnosed, most commonly attested diagnosis is unipolar depression. Unfortunately, even today, few mental health professionals know the picture well enough and can provide adequate guidance to lessen the distress of the patient, their relatives and friends.

The diagnosis of TB is treacherous: the signs and symptoms can have numerous manifestations in the same patient; as well as vary greatly from one person to another. In general, people with Bipolar Disorder have difficulty dedicating themselves to a professional career, maintaining productivity and balance in their emotional lives, and cultivating lasting relationships. Those affected by the disorder do not always have control of what they say during the periods of illness. Drug treatment is fundamental and complex because it requires two strategies: prophylaxis (prevention of seizures) and control of acute symptoms; the psychological accompaniment is fundamental for a good long-term evolution.

The good news is that the proper approach can ensure a virtually normal life, especially if the disease is diagnosed early. But the earlier and deeper the patient and his family understand TB, the greater the chance they can control the disease and make its consequences less harmful. And in this case, the information can be considered a fundamental part of the people involved in the situation being informed that TB is a chronic disease with biological (genetic and other) causes associated with environmental factors.

It is understandable, therefore, that the status of mental illness of Bipolar Disorder is often questioned. After all, the patient experiences common exacerbated reactions that a healthy person could also have. Anyone is, for example, able to react angrily in the face of frustration or injustice. However, the bipolar patient may become depressed or overly aggressive. A lot of people have also spent a little more money than they intended or were pissed at having received bad news. However, the person with TB spends enormous amounts without any planning, to the point of getting involved in debt to buy products that he does not need or, on receiving unpleasant news, he stays in bed.

But how can exacerbated reactions distinguish one person with Bipolar Disorder from others? Was it not just a peculiar reaction of each individual, purely psychological, without result of some injury or failure in brain functioning? Currently, the World Health Organization (WHO, 2009) recognizes Bipolar Disorder as a disease. To be known in this way, the picture must have well-established organic causes; its evolution in time and physical implications should be known, as well as the possibilities of treating the symptoms. The greatest difficulty, however, is to define their limits, which depend on clinical evaluations based on symptoms and signs, once they can give the definitive diagnosis of Bipolar Disorder.

The main characteristic of TB is the instability of various brain functions, which can be noticed in mood alteration, ranging from deep sadness to excessive joy, showing in the anxiety and irritability that in a short time can turn into apathy. These variations appear to be associated with instability of brain functioning, both in information storage (memory) and in attention control (excessive distraction).

There is variation from pessimism to uncontrollable optimism, and the speed of thought can increase or decrease. Changes in sleep and appetite, both for excess and for lack, are also common. In these situations, hormonal systems often become disorganized, reflecting a chaotic or cyclic biological rhythm, and often the patient switches overnight. There is also an excessive decrease or increase of energy.

The same is true for the ability to feel pleasure. The most curious thing is that humorous change can occur in a few hours, or in a few days - and sometimes last for weeks, months or even years. Therefore, there are patients who are bipolar and stay for long periods in the same state, which is usually depressive. In these cases, when examining any moment in the life of this patient, the impression is that there is no instability, although it may have occurred in the past or simply been represented by a single change, from the state considered normal for the depressive .

A new question arises: if instability is the central feature of Bipolar Disorder, should healthy people be unstable without great expressions of sadness or joy? This question leads to interesting reflection. The human body has control systems that prevent the various functions from being excessively outside the so-called minimum parameters for, for example, sleep time or levels of physical and mental activity. The variability is critical for the human being to adapt to environmental situations that change frequently and require accommodations such as eventually sleeping later to attend a social event or finish writing an article. In the TB patient's body these control systems function inadequately, which allows for "leaks" and leads to uncontrolled, ultimately disrupting other bodily functions.

People who are considered healthy tend to have small variations in body functions, which adapt to the demands of the environment, while bipolar patients have major changes that become incompatible with external events. It is therefore quite acceptable (and even a sign of mental health) to feel, acknowledge and express joy and sadness, to varying degrees, provided that these feelings, triggered by external or subjective factors, apply to the context - and have intensity compatible with situation in the case of patients with TB - the more the functions that regulate mood states are disorganized, the more serious and complex the clinical presentation is.

According to the Diagnostic and Statistical Manual of Mental Disorders (DSM) to diagnose Bipolar Disorder Type I, it is necessary to fulfill the following criteria for a manic episode. The manic episode may have been preceded or followed by major hypomanic or depressive episodes.

Diagnostic Criteria for Manic Episode

A. A distinct period of abnormal and persistently high, expansive or irritable mood and abnormal and persistent increase in goal-directed or energy activity, lasting at least one week and present most of the day, almost every day (or any duration if hospitalization is required).

B. During the period of mood disturbance and increased energy or activity, three (or more) of the following symptoms (four if mood is only irritable) are present to a significant degree and represent a remarkable change from usual behavior:

1) Inflated self-esteem or grandiosity.

2) Reduced need for sleep (eg, feel rested with only three hours of sleep).

3) Quieter than usual or pressure to keep talking.

4) Leak of ideas or subjective experience that thoughts are accelerated.

5) Distractibility (eg, attention is too easily diverted by insignificant or irrelevant external stimuli), as reported or observed.

6) Increase in activity directed to goals (whether socially, at work or school, or sexually) or psychomotor agitation (activity without non-objective purpose).

7) Excessive involvement in activities with high potential for painful consequences (eg, involvement in unrestrained buying sprees, sexual indiscretions or foolish financial investments).

C. The mood disturbance is serious enough to cause severe impairment in social, occupational or hospital functioning in order to prevent harm to oneself or others, or there are psychotic features.

D. The episode is not attributable to the physiological effects of a substance (eg, drug of abuse, drug, other treatment) or other medical condition.

Note 1: A complete manic episode that arises during antidepressant treatment (eg, medication, electroconvulsive therapy) but which persists at a level of signs and symptoms beyond the physiological effect of this treatment is sufficient evidence for a manic episode and therefore for a diagnosis of Type B Bipolar Disorder. **Note 2**: The AD Criteria represent a manic episode. At least one manic episode in life is required for the diagnosis of Bipolar Disorder Type I.

Source: Diagnostic and Statistical Manual of Mental Disorders. (APA, 2018).

Associated Features that Support Diagnosis

During a manic episode, individuals often do not realize they are sick or in need of treatment, resisting vehemently attempts at treatment. They can change the way they dress, makeup or personal appearance to an extravagant style and / or with greater sexual appeal. Some perceive greater olfactory, auditory or visual acuity. Gambling and antisocial behavior may accompany the manic episode. There are people who can become hostile and physically threatening to others and, when delusional, may physically assault or commit suicide. The catastrophic consequences of a manic episode (eg, involuntary hospitalization, difficulties with justice, serious financial difficulties) usually result from impaired critical judgment, loss of insight, and hyperactivity. Mood can change quickly to anger or depression. Depressive symptoms may occur during a manic episode and, when present, last for hours, hours or, more rarely, days.

Diagnostic Features

The essential feature of a manic episode is a distinct period of abnormal and persistently high, expansive or irritable mood and persistent increase in activities lasting at least one week and present most of the day, almost every day (or any duration, if hospitalization becomes necessary), accompanied by at least three additional Criterion B symptoms. If mood is irritable rather than elevated or expansive, at least four Criterion B symptoms should be present.

Humor in a manic episode is often described as euphoric, overly cheerful, elevated, or "feeling on top of the world." In some cases, humor is so abnormally contagious that it is easily recognized as excessive and can be characterized by unlimited and indiscriminate enthusiasm for interpersonal, sexual, or professional interactions. By Mémjplo, one can spontaneously initiate long conversations with strangers in public. Sometimes the predominant mood is irritable rather than elevated, particularly when the individual's desires are denied or when he has been using substances. Rapid changes in mood over short periods of time may occur, being referred to as lability (alternation between euphoria, dysphoria and irritability). In children, happiness, folly and "stupidity" are normal in the context of special occasions; if these symptoms are recurrent, inadequate to the context and beyond what is expected for the child's level of development, they may satisfy Criterion A. If happiness is unusual for the child (other than usual) and the mood change occurs concomitantly to symptoms that satisfy Criterion B for mania, increases diagnostic certainty; the change in mood should, however, be accompanied by a persistent increase in activity or energy, which is evident to those who know the child well.

During the manic episode, one can get involved in several new projects at the same time. Projects are usually started with little knowledge of the topic, and nothing seems to be beyond the reach of the individual. Increased activity levels may manifest at unusual times of the day.

Inflated self-esteem is usually present, varying from self-confidence without criticism to accentuated grandiosity, and can reach delirious proportions (Crit B1). Despite the lack of any particular experience or talent, the individual can begin complex tasks such as writing a novel or seeking publicity for some impractical invention. Delusions of grandeur (eg, having a special relationship with a famous person) are common. In children, over-valuing skills and belief that, for example, they may be the best in sports or the smartest in the classroom are common; when, however, these beliefs are present despite clear evidence to the contrary, or the child tries clearly dangerous acts and, more importantly, represents a change of his habitual behavior, the criterion of grandiosity must be satisfied.

One of the most common features is the reduction of sleep need (Criterion B2), which differs from insomnia, in which the individual wants to sleep or feels the need for it, but can not. He can sleep little if he can, or he can wake up several hours earlier than usual, feeling rested and full of energy. When the sleep disorder is severe, the individual can go without sleep for days and have no tiredness. Often, reducing the need for sleep heralds the onset of a manic episode.

Speech can be rapid, depressed, loud and difficult to interrupt (Criterion B3). Individuals can speak continuously and without concern for other people's communication desires, often in an invasive manner or without attention to the relevance of what is said. Sometimes speech is characterized by jokes, puns, amusing nonsense and theatricality, with dramatic mannerisms, singing, and excessive gestures. The intensity and tone of speech are often more important than what is being transmitted. When humor is more irritable than expansive, speech can be marked by complaints, hostile comments or angry tirades, especially if attempts are made to interrupt the individual. Symptoms of Criteria A and Criterion B may be accompanied by symptoms of the opposite pole (depressive) (see the "mixed characteristics" specifier).

Often, the individual's thoughts flow at a speed greater than that which can be expressed in speech (Criterion B4). There is often an escape of ideas, evidenced by an almost continuous flow of accelerated speech, with sudden changes from one topic to another. When brainstorming is severe, speech may become disorganized, incoherent and particularly distressing to the individual. Thoughts are sometimes felt to be so overcrowded that it is difficult to speak.

Distractibility (Criterion B5) is evidenced by an inability to filter irrelevant external stimuli (eg, interviewer clothing, background noise or conversations, room furniture), and often does not allow Manic episode keep a rational conversation or respect directions. Increased goal-oriented activity often involves over-planning and engaging in multiple activities, including sexual, professional, political, or religious activities. Increased sexual drive, fantasy, and behavior are often present. Individuals in a manic episode often show increased sociability (eg, renewing old friendships or phoning friends or even strangers), without concern for the uncomfortable, domineering, and demanding nature of these interactions. They often exhibit psychomotor agitation or restlessness (activity without a purpose), walking from side to side or holding multiple conversations simultaneously. There are those who write too many letters, e-mails, text messages, etc., on various subjects to friends, public figures, or the media.

The criterion of increased activity may be difficult to ascertain in children; when the child assumes several tasks simultaneously, begins to elaborate plans that are complicated and unrealistic for projects, develops previously absent and inadequate developmental concerns (not justified by sexual abuse or exposure to explicit sex material), Criterion B can be satisfied based on clinical judgment. It is crucial to determine whether the behavior represents a mu for the required period of time; and if it occurs in temporal association with other symptoms of mania.

Excessive moodiness, excessive optimism, grandiosity, and impaired critical judgment often lead to reckless involvement in activities such as shopping sprees, donations of personal belongings, reckless driving, foolish financial investments, and sexual promiscuity unusual to the individual, even when such activities can lead to catastrophic consequences (Criterion B7). The individual can acquire many unnecessary items without having the money to pay for them and in some cases donate those items. Sexual behavior may include infidelity or indiscriminate sexual encounters with strangers, generally without regard to the risk of sexually transmitted diseases or interpersonal consequences.

The manic episode should cause severe impairment in social or occupational functioning or require hospitalization to prevent harm to yourself or others (eg, financial loss, illegal activity, job loss, self-defeating behavior). By definition, the presence of psychotic features during a manic episode also satisfies Criterion C.

Signs or symptoms of mania that are attributed to the physiological effects of a drug of abuse (eg in the context of cocaine or amphetamine poisoning), side effects of medications or treatments (eg, steroids, L-dopa , antidepressants, stimulants) or other medical condition do not warrant the diagnosis of Bipolar I Type 1 disorder. A complete manic episode, however, which arose during treatment (eg medication, electroconvulsive therapy, phototherapy) or drug use and persists in addition to the physiological effect of the inducing agent (after the drug is completely absent from the individual's organism or the expected effects of the electroconvulsive therapy are completely dissipated) is sufficient evidence for a diagnosis and manic episode (Criterion D).

Caution is advised so that one or more symptoms (mainly increased irritability, nervousness, or agitation after use of antidepressants) are not considered sufficient for the diagnosis of a manic or hypomanic episode nor necessarily an indication of bipolar diathesis. It is necessary to fulfill the criteria for a manic episode for the diagnosis of Bipolar Disorder type I, but there is no need for major hypomanic or depressive episodes. They may, however, precede or follow a manic episode. Complete descriptions of the diagnostic characteristics of a hypomanic episode can be found in the text of Bipolar D-type disorder, and the characteristics of a major depressive episode are described in the text on major depressive disorder.

Prevalence

The estimated 12-month prevalence in the United States was 0.6% for Type I Bipolar Disorder as defined in DSM-V. The 12-month prevalence of the disorder in 11 countries ranged from 0.0 to 0.6%. The ratio of lifetime prevalence among males and females is approximately 1.1: 1.

Development and Course

The mean age at onset of the first manic, hypomanic or major depressive episode is about 18 years for Type I Bipolar Disorder. Special considerations are needed for the diagnosis in children. Since children of the same age may be in different developmental stages, it is difficult to precisely define what is "normal" or "expected" at a given point. Thus, each child should be considered according to their usual behavior. The onset occurs throughout the life cycle, including the first symptoms can start at 60 or 70 years. The onset of manic symptoms (eg, sexual or social disinhibition) at the end of adulthood or in senescence should indicate the possibility of medical conditions (eg, frontotemporal neurocognitive disorder) and substance ingestion or withdrawal.

Over 90% of individuals who have had a single episode of mania have recurrent episodes of mood swings. About 60% of manic episodes occur immediately before a major depressive episode. People with Type I Bipolar Disorder who had multiple episodes (four or more) of mood (major depressive, manic or hypomanic) in one year receive the "fast cycling" specifier.

Risk Factors and Prognosis

Environmental Bipolar disorder is more common in countries with high incomes than those with lower incomes (1.4 vs. 0.7%). Separated, divorced, or widowed individuals have higher rates of Type I Bipolar Disorder than those who are married or never married, but the sense in which the association changes is unclear.

Genetic and physiological. Family history of Bipolar Disorder is one of the strongest and most consistent risk factors for disorders of this category. There is, on average, a 10-fold higher risk among adult relatives of individuals with type I and type II bipolar disorders. The magnitude of the risk increases with the degree of kinship. Schizophrenia and Bipolar Disorder probably share a genetic origin, reflected in the family coaggregation of schizophrenia and Bipolar Disorder.

Course Modifiers. After a person has had a manic episode with psychotic features, subsequent manic episodes are more likely to include psychotic features. Incomplete recovery between episodes is more common when the current episode is accompanied by psychotic features incongruent with mood.

Diagnostic Issues Concerning Culture

There is little information on specific cultural differences in the presentation of Type I Bipolar Disorder. One possible explanation for this may be that diagnostic tools are often translated and applied in different cultures without cross-cultural validation. In a North American study, the 12-month prevalence of Type I Bipolar Disorder was significantly lower for Afro-Caribbean than for African Americans or whites.

Gender-Related Diagnostic Issues

Female subjects are more susceptible to rapid and mixed cycling states and to comorbid patterns that differ from males, including higher rates of eating disorders throughout life. Individuals with Bipolar I or Type II Bipolar Disorder are more likely to have depressive symptoms. They also have a higher lifetime risk of alcohol use disorder than males and an even greater likelihood of alcohol use disorder than females in the general population.

Suicide Risk

The risk of life-threatening suicide in people with Bipolar Disorder is estimated at least 15 times that of the general population. In fact, Bipolar Disorder can account for a quarter of all suicides. Previous history of attempted suicide and the percentage of days spent in depression in the previous year are associated with increased risk of suicide attempts and success in those attempts.

Functional Consequences of Type I Bipolar Disorder

Although many individuals with Bipolar Disorder return to a fully functional level between episodes, approximately 30% show significant impairment in professional functioning. Functional recovery is far from recovering from symptoms, especially in relation to the recovery of professional functioning, resulting in lower socioeconomic status despite equivalent levels of education, when compared to the general population. Individuals with Type I Bipolar Disorder perform worse than healthy people on cognitive tests. Cognitive impairments can contribute to occupational and interpersonal difficulties and persist throughout life, even during euthymic periods.

Differential Diagnosis

Major depressive disorder. Major depressive disorder may also be accompanied by hypomanic or manic symptoms (fewer symptoms or for a shorter period than is necessary for mania or hypomania). When the individual presents in an episode of major depression, one must watch for previous episodes of mania or hypomania. Symptoms of irritability may be associated with major depressive disorder or Bipolar Disorder, increasing the diagnostic complexity.

Other bipolar disorders. The diagnosis of Type I Bipolar Disorder differs from that of Type II Bipolar Disorder because of the presence of an earlier episode of mania. Other Bipolar Disorder and related disorders specified or Bipolar Disorder and related unspecified disorders should be distinguished from type I and type II bipolar disorders, considering whether episodes with manic or hypomanic symptoms or episodes with depressive symptoms fully meet criteria for those conditions.

A Bipolar Disorder due to another medical condition can be distinguished from type I and type II bipolar disorders by identifying, based on the best clinical evidence, a causal medical condition.

Generalized Anxiety Disorder (GAD), Panic Disorder, Post-traumatic Stress Disorder (PTSD) or others anxiety disorders. These disorders should be considered in the differential diagnosis both as primary disorder and, in some cases, as a comorbid disorder. A careful clinical history is needed to differentiate generalized anxiety disorder from Bipolar Disorder, since anxious ruminations can be confused with accelerated thoughts, and efforts to minimize feelings of anxiety can be understood as impulsive behavior. In the same way, symptoms of posttraumatic stress disorder need to be differentiated from Bipolar Disorder. It is useful to consider the episodic nature of the described symptoms, as well as to evaluate possible triggers of the symptoms, when this differential diagnosis is made.

Bipolar disorder induced by substance / drug. Substance-related disorders may manifest with substance / drug induced manic symptoms and need to be differentiated from Type I Bipolar Disorder. The response to mood stabilizers during substance / drug-induced mania may not necessarily be sufficient to diagnose a disorder Bipolar. There may be substantial overlap with the tendency of people with Type I Bipolar Disorder to overuse substances during an episode. A primary diagnosis of Bipolar Disorder should be established based on the symptoms that persist after the substances are no longer being used.

Attention Deficit Hyperactivity Disorder (ADHD). This disorder may be misdiagnosed as Bipolar Disorder, especially in adolescents and children. There are many symptoms overlapping with the symptoms of mania, such as rapid speech, fast thoughts, distractibility and less need for sleep. "Double counting" of symptoms related to both ADHD and Bipolar Disorder can be avoided if the clinician clarifies if the symptom (s) represents a distinct episode.

Personality disorders. Personality disorders, such as Borderline Personality Disorder, may have substantial symptomatic overlap with bipolar disorders, since mood lability and impulsivity are common in both conditions. For the diagnosis of Bipolar Disorder, the symptoms should represent a distinct episode and a remarkable increase in relation to the habitual behavior of the individual. There should be no diagnosis of personality disorder during untreated mood episode.

Disorders with marked irritability. In individuals with significant irritability, especially children and adolescents, care should be taken to diagnose Bipolar Disorder only to those who have had a clear episode of mania or hypomania, that is, a distinct period of time, with the necessary duration, during which the irritability was clearly different from the habitual behavior of the individual and was accompanied by the onset of the symptoms of Criterion B. When the irritability of a child is persistent and particularly severe, it is more appropriate. The diagnosis of disruptive disorder of mood deregulation. In fact, when any child is being evaluated for mania, it is critical that the symptoms represent an unambiguous change in their typical behavior.

Comorbidity

Comorbid mental disorders are common, with anxiety disorders (eg, panic attacks, anxiety disorder, social phobia, specific phobia) occurring in about three quarters of individuals. Any disruptive disorder, ADHD, 1 disorder of impulse control or conduct (eg, intermittent explosive disorder, oppositional defiant disorder, conduct disorder) and any substance use disorder (eg, use disorder of alcohol) occur in more than half of individuals with Type I Bipolar Disorder. Adults with Type I Bipolar Disorder have high rates of serious and / or untreated comorbid medical conditions. Metabolic syndrome and migraine are more common among people with Bipolar Disorder than in the general population. More than half of people whose symptoms meet the criteria for Bipolar Disorder have an alcohol use disorder, and those with both disorders are at high risk of attempting suicide.

Diagnostic Criteria for Hypomanic Episode

A. A distinct period of abnormal and persistently high, expansive or irritable mood and abnormal and persistent increase in activity or energy, lasting at least four consecutive days and present most of the day, most days.

B. During the period of mood disturbance and increased energy and activity, three (or more) of the following symptoms (four if mood is only irritable) persist, represent a noticeable change from usual be-havior, and are present to a significant degree :

1) Inflated self-esteem or grandiosity.

2) Reduced need for sleep (eg, feel rested with only three hours of sleep).

3) Quieter than usual or pressure to keep talking.

4) Leak of ideas or subjective experience that thoughts are accelerated.

5) Distractibility (attention is easily diverted by insignificant or irrelevant external stimuli) as reported or observed.

6) Increase in activity directed to goals (whether socially, at work or school, or sexually) or psychomotor agitation.

7) Excessive involvement in activities with high potential for painful consequences (eg, involvement in unrestrained buying sprees, sexual indiscretions or foolish financial investments).

C. The episode is associated with a clear change in functioning that is not characteristic of the individual when asymptomatic.

D. Mood disturbance and change in functioning are observable by others.

E The episode is not serious enough to cause severe impairment in social or occupational functioning or to require hospitalization. If there are psychotic features, by definition, the episode is manic.

F. The episode is not attributable to the physiological effects of a substance (eg, drug of abuse, medication, other treatment).

____

Note: 1. A complete hypomanic episode that arises during antidepressant treatment (eg medication, electroconvulsive therapy) but persists at a level of signs and symptoms beyond the physiological effect of this treatment is sufficient evidence for a hypomanic episode diagnosis. However, caution is advised that 1 or 2 symptoms (mainly increased irritability, nervousness, or agitation after use of antidepressants) are not considered sufficient for the diagnosis of hypomanic episode nor necessarily indicative of a bipolar diathesis. **Note: 2**. Criteria A-F represents a hypomanic episode. These episodes are common in Type I Bipolar Disorder, although not necessary for the diagnosis of this disorder.

Source: Diagnostic and Statistical Manual of Mental Disorders, (APA, 2018)

Major Depressive Episode

A. Five (or more) of the following symptoms were present during the same two week period and represent a change from previous functioning; At least one of the symptoms is **(1)** depressed mood or **(2)** loss of interest or pleasure. **Note**: Do not include symptoms that are clearly attributable to another medical condition.

1) Depressed mood most of the day, almost every day, as indicated by subjective report (eg, feels sad, empty or hopeless) or by observation by another person (eg, it seems tearful). (**Note**: In children and adolescents, it can be irritable mood).

2) Decreased interest or pleasure in all or most of the activities most of the day, almost every day (as indicated by a subjective report or observation made by another person).

3) Significant loss or weight loss without dieting (eg, change of more than 5% of body weight in one month) or reduced or in-

creased appetite almost every day. (**Note**: In children, consider failure to achieve expected weight gain.)

4) Insomnia or hypersomnia almost daily.

5) Psychomotor agitation or retardation almost every day (observable by other people, not merely subjective feelings of restlessness or being slowed down).

6) Fatigue or loss of energy almost every day.

7) Feelings of worthlessness or excessive or inappropriate guilt (which may be delusional) almost every day (not merely self-recrimination or guilt for being ill).

8) Decreased ability to think or concentrate, or indecision almost every day (by subjective report or observation made by another person).

9) Recurrent thoughts of death (not only fear of dying), recurrent suicidal ideation without a specific plan, suicide attempt or specific plan to commit suicide.

B. The symptoms cause clinically significant distress or impairment in social, occupational, or other important areas of life.

C. The episode is not attributable to the physiological effects of a substance or other medical condition

---

Note 1: Criteria A-C represents a major depressive episode. This type of episode is common in Type I Bipolar Disorder, although it is not necessary for the diagnosis of this disorder. **Note 2**: Responses to a significant loss (eg mourning, financial ruin, natural disaster losses, severe medical illness or disability) may include intense feelings of sadness, rumination About loss, insomnia, lack of appetite, and loss of appetite. observed in Criterion A, which may resemble a depressive episode. Although such symptoms may be understood or considered appropriate to loss, the presence of a major depressive episode in addition to the normal response to a significant loss should also be carefully considered. This decision inevitably demands the exercise of clinical judgment, based on the history of the individual and cultural norms for the expression of suffering in the context of a loss.

Source: Diagnostic and Statistical Manual of Mental Disorders. (APA, 2018)

Diagnostic Features

Type II Bipolar Disorder is characterized by a clinical course of recurrent mood episodes consisting of one or more major depressive episodes (CA Criteria in "Major Depressive Episode") and at least one hypomanic episode (AF Criteria in "Hypomanic Episode"). The major depressive episode should last at least two weeks, and the hypomanic episode should be at least four days long in order to meet the diagnostic criteria. During the mood episode (s), the required amount of symptoms should be present for most of the day, almost every day, and the symptoms represent a remarkable change in behavior and behavior. The presence of a manic episode during the course of the disease excludes the diagnosis of Bipolar Disorder type II (Criterion B in "Bipolar Disorder Type II").

Episodes of substance / drug-induced depressive disorder or Bipolar Disorder and substance / drug-related related disorder (due to the physiological effects of a drug, other somatic treatments for depression, drugs of abuse or toxin exposure) or depressive disorder and related disorder due to another medical condition or Bipolar Disorder and related disorder due to another medical condition do not count towards the diagnosis of Type II Bipolar Disorder unless they persist beyond the physiological effects of the treatment or substance and meet the duration criteria for an episode. In addition, episodes should not be better accounted for by schizoaffective disorder, not overlapping with schizophrenia, schizophreniform disorder, delusional disorder or other spectrum disorder of schizophrenia or other specified psychotic disorders or with spectrum disorder schizophrenia and other disorders psychotic disorder (Criterion C in "Bipolar Disorder Type II").

Depressive episodes or hypomanic oscillations should cause clinically significant distress or impairment in social, occupational, or other important areas of life (Criterion D in "Bipolar D-type Disorder"); for hypomanic episodes, however, this requirement need not be met. A haemorrhagic episode that causes significant impairment could be diagnosed as a manic episode and diagnosis of type I Bipolar Disorder throughout life. Recurrent major depressive episodes are more frequent and prolonged than those occurring in Type I Bipolar Disorder.

People with Type II Bipolar Disorder usually present themselves to the clinician during a major depressive episode and are unlikely to initially complain of hypomania. In general, hypomanic episodes do not cause harm by themselves. Instead, impairment is a consequence of major depressive episodes or the persistent pattern of changes and swings, unpredictable mood and unstable interpersonal or occupational functioning. Individuals with Type II Bipolar Disorder may not regard hypomanic episodes as pathological or harmful, although other people may feel disturbed by their behavior. Straight. Clinical information provided by other people, such as close friends or relatives, is often helpful in establishing a diagnosis of Bipolar Disorder type II.

A hypomanic episode should not be confused with the various days of euthymia and restoration of energy or activity that may come after remission of a major depressive episode. Despite the substantial differences in duration and severity between a manic episode and a hypomanic episode, Bipolar Disorder Type II does not represent a "milder form" of Type I Bipolar Disorder. Compared with individuals with Type B Bipolar Disorder, those with Bipolar Disorder type II have greater chronicity of the disease and spend, on average, more time in the depressive phase, which can be severe and / or incapacitating.

Depressive symptoms during a hypomanic episode or hypomanic symptoms during a depressive episode are common in individuals with Type II Bipolar Disorder and are more common in females, especially hypomania with mixed characteristics. Individuals with hypomania with mixed characteristics may not characterize their symptoms as hypomania, experiencing them as depression with increased energy or irritability.

Associated Features that Support Diagnosis

A common feature of Type II Bipolar Disorder is impulsivity, which may contribute to suicide attempts and substance use disorders. Impulsiveness may also arise from a comorbid personality disorder, substance use disorder, anxiety disorder, another mental disorder, or a medical condition. There may be increased levels of creativity in some individuals with Bipolar Disorder. The relationship may be, however, non-linear; that is, great creative accomplishments in life have been associated with milder forms of Bipolar Disorder, and superior creativity has been identified in unaffected family members. The individual's satisfaction with increased creativity during hypomanic episodes may contribute to ambivalence about seeking treatment or impairing adherence to it.

Prevalence

The prevalence in 12 months of Bipolar Disorder type II, internationally, is of 0.3%. In the United States, the prevalence at 12 months is 0.8%. The prevalence rate of Bipolar Disorder type II pediatric is difficult to establish. In DSM-IV, bipolar type I, bipolar type II and bipolar disorders without other specifications resulted in a combined prevalence rate of 1.8% in samples from communities in the United States and abroad, with higher rates (2.7% including) in young people who are 12 years of age or older.

Development and Course

Although Type II Bipolar Disorder can begin in late adolescence and during adulthood, the mean age of onset occurs around age 25, which is somewhat later in comparison to Type I Bipolar Disorder and earlier in comparison to major depressive disorder. Typically, the disease begins with a depressive episode and is not recognized as Bipolar Disorder type II until the onset of a hypomanic episode, which occurs in about 12% of people with initial diagnosis of major depressive disorder. Anxiety disorder, by use of substance or eating disorder may also precede the diagnosis, complicating its detection. Many individuals have several episodes of major depression prior to the identification of the first hypomanic episode.

The number of episodes in life (hypomanic and major depressives) tends to be higher for Type II Bipolar Disorder compared to major depressive disorder or Type I Bipolar Disorder. However, individuals with Bipolar I Disorder are actually more likely to have Hypomanic symptoms than those with Type II Bipolar Disorder. The interval between mood episodes, in the course of a Type II Bipolar Disorder, tends to decrease with aging. While the hypomanic episode is the defining characteristic of Bipolar Disorder type II, depressive episodes are more enduring and incapacitating over time. Despite the predominance of depression, a hypomanic episode occurs, the diagnosis becomes Bipolar Disorder type II and never reverts to major depressive disorder.

Approximately 5 to 15% of individuals with Type II Bipolar Disorder have multiple (four or more) mood episodes (hypomanic or major depressive) in the previous 12 months. When present, this pattern is recorded by the "fast cycling" specifier. By definition, psychotic symptoms do not occur in hypomanic episodes and appear to be less frequent in major depressive episodes of Type II Bipolar Disorder than in those of Type I Bipolar Disorder.

Moving from a depressive episode to a manic or hypomanic (with or without mixed characteristics) can occur both spontaneously and during treatment for depression. About 5 to 15% of individuals with Bipolar Disorder type II end up developing a manic episode, which changes the diagnosis for Type I Bipolar Disorder, regardless of the later course.

It is a challenge to make the diagnosis in children, especially those with non episodic irritability and hyperexcitability (absence of well-defined periods of altered mood). Non-episodic irritability in young people is associated with increased risk for anxicty disorders and major depressive disorder but not Bipolar Disorder in adult life. Persistently irritable youth have lower familial rates of Bipolar Disorder compared to young people with Bipolar Disorder. For the diagnosis of a hypomanic episode, the child's symptoms should exceed what is expected in a given environment and culture for their stage of development. Compared with early adulthood, the onset of Bipolar Disorder Type II in childhood or adolescence may be associated with a more severe course throughout life. The three-year incidence rate for the onset of Bipolar Disorder Type II in adults over 60 years of age is 0.34%. However, distinguishing individuals over 60 with early or late onset type II bipolar disorder does not appear to have any clinical utility.

Genetic and physiological risk and prognostic factors

The risk of Type II Bipolar Disorder tends to be higher among relatives of people with this condition, as opposed to people with Type I Bipolar Disorder or major depressive disorder. There may be genetic factors influencing the age of onset of bipolar disorders. The risk of suicide in Bipolar Disorder type II. About one-third of individuals with iranstoma report a history of suicide attempt throughout life. Prevalence rates of attempted lifetime in bipolar type I and type II disorders appear to be similar (32.4 and 36.3%, respectively).

The lethality of the attempts, however, defined by a smaller proportion of attempts until consummate suicides, may be higher in individuals with Type II Bipolar Disorder compared to those with Type I Bipolar Disorder. There may be association between genetic markers and increased risk of suicidal behavior in individuals with Bipolar Disorder, including a 6.5-fold greater risk of suicide among first-degree relatives of probands with type II Bipolar Disorder compared to those with Type I Bipolar Disorder.

Functional Consequences of Type II Bipolar Disorder

Although many people with Bipolar Disorder type II return to a fully functional level between mood episodes, at least 15% continue to have some dysfunction between episodes, and 20% change directly to another episode of mood without recovery between episodes. Functional recovery is far from recovering from the symptoms of Bipolar Disorder type II, especially with regard to professional recovery, resulting in lower socioeconomic status despite equivalent levels of education compared to the general population. Individuals with Type II Bipolar Disorder have poorer performance than those with healthy cognitive tests and, except in memory and semantic fluency, have similar cognitive impairment to those with Type I Bipolar Disorder. Cognitive impairments associated with Type II Bipolar Disorder may contribute to difficulties at work. Prolonged unemployment in individuals with Bipolar Disorder is associated with more episodes of depression, older age, higher rates of current panic disorder, and history of lifelong alcohol use disorder.

Differential Diagnosis

Major depressive disorder. Perhaps the most challenging differential diagnosis to consider is that of major depressive disorder, which may be accompanied by hypomanic or manic symptoms that do not meet all of the criteria (fewer symptoms or shorter duration than needed for a hypomanic episode). This is especially true in the evaluation of people with symptoms of irritability, which may be associated with major depressive disorder or Type II Bipolar Disorder.

Cyclothymic disorder. In cyclothymic disorder, there are several periods of hypomanic symptoms and innumerable periods of depressive symptoms that do not meet the criteria of symptom numbers or duration for major depressive episode. Type II bipolar disorder is different from cyclothymic disorder due to the presence of one or more depressive episodes. When a major depressive episode occurs after the first two years of cyclothymic disorder, the additional diagnosis of Type II Bipolar Disorder is established.

Spectrum disorders of schizophrenia and other related psychotic disorders. Type II Bipolar Disorder should be differentiated from psychotic disorders (eg, schizoaffective disorder, schizophrenia, and delusional disorder). Schizophrenia, schizoaffective disorder and delusional disorder are all characterized by periods of psychotic symptoms that occur in the absence of marked mood symptoms. Other useful considerations include the associated symptoms, the previous course and the family history.

Panic disorder and others anxiety disorders. Anxiety disorders need to be taken into account in differential diagnosis and may often be present as comorbid disorders.

Substance use disorders. Substance use disorders are part of the differential diagnosis. Attention Deficit / Hyperactivity Disorder. Attention Deficit / Hyperactivity Disorder may be misdiagnosed as Type II Bipolar Disorder, especially in adolescents and children. Many symptoms of ADHD, such as speed of speech, speed of thoughts, distractibility and less need for sleep, overlap with those of hypomania. The "double counting" of symptoms for ADHD and Bipolar Disorder type II can be avoided if the clinician clarifies if the symptoms represent a distinct episode and if the remarkable increase in relation to the habitual behavior of the individual, necessary for the diagnosis of Bipolar Disorder type II , is present.

Personality disorders. The same convention applied to ADHD applies to the assessment of an individual for personality disorder, such as borderline personality disorder, since mood swings and im-pulsivity are common in personality disorders and Bipolar D-type Disorder. symptoms should represent a distinct episode, and the re-markable increase in relation to the habitual behavior of the individu-al, necessary for the diagnosis of Bipolar Disorder type n, should be present. There should be no diagnosis of personality disorder during untreated mood episode, unless the life history supports the presence of a personality disorder.

Other bipolar disorders. Diagnosis of Type II Bipolar Disorder should be differentiated from Type I Bipolar Disorder by the careful evaluation of whether or not past episodes of mania have occurred. It must be differentiated from other Bipolar Disorder and related disorders specified or Bipolar Disorder and related disorder not specified by confirmation of the presence of complete episodes of hypomania and depression.

Comorbidity

Type II Bipolar Disorder is very often associated with one or more of a comorbid mental disorder, with anxiety disorders being the most common. About 60% of people with type Bipolar Disorder have three or more comorbid mental disorders; 75% have anxiety disorder; and 37%, substance use disorder. Children and adolescents with Type II Bipolar Disorder have a higher rate of comorbid anxiety disorders compared to those with Type I Bipolar Disorder, and anxiety disorder occurs more frequently before Bipolar Disorder. Anxiety disorder and substance use disorders occur in individuals with Type II Bipolar Disorder in a higher proportion than in the general population. About 14% of people with type Bipolar Disorder have at least one lifelong eating disorder, with binge eating disorder being more common than bulimia nervosa and anorexia nervosa. These comorbid disorders generally do not seem to follow a course that is actually independent of that of Bipolar Disorder; have, however, strong associations with states of humor. For example, anxiety disorders and eating disorders tend to associate more with depressive symptoms, and substance use disorders are moderately associated with manic symptoms.

Differential Diagnostics

Mania, particularly in the more severe forms associated with paranoid delusions, agitation and irritability, may be difficult to distinguish from schizophrenia, which in general has a greater number of delusions incongruent with mood and first-order Schneider's symptoms (eg, , auditory hallucinations referring to the patient in the third person), as well as negative symptoms, such as affective blunting. Delusional ideas of grandeur may also appear in schizophrenia, but without the expansive or euphoric mood observed in the mania. Hypomania can be confused with normal mood states such as joy and irritability that often have positive or negative triggering factors (such as good or bad news) that are not necessarily perceived by others as different from the person's usual mood pattern , do not cause harm, nor do they involve involvement with risk activities or decrease in the need for sleep.

Hypomania may or may not have triggering factors, which may be positive or negative, such as the death of the spouse. Often, hypomania and Type II Bipolar Disorder can be confused with personality disorders, such as antisocial, narcissistic, histrionic and borderline. The DSM-V solves the problem of this differential diagnosis allowing the comorbidity of these frames. Personality disorders are usually more chronic, beginning in childhood or adolescence and have a worse response to drug treatment. The family history of mood disorder also helps in differential diagnosis. (MORENO, 2005)

According to Akiskal et al. (2001), mania and hypomania with irritability should be differentiated from unipolar depression. In this, if there is psychomotor agitation, it is not as intense as in TB. Depressive moods are usually present most of the time in depression, not hypomania or mania. The differential diagnosis should also be made with anxious disorders that usually accompany depressions, such as generalized anxiety. According to this same author, manias can also be characterized by anxious mood. Again the agitation of generalized anxiety is less than that of mania. Family history of TB also helps in differential diagnosis.

Impulse control disorders such as kleptomania, pyromania and intermittent explosive disorder should be distinguished from hypomania and mania. In general, these are characterized only by lack of control of impulsivity, with no complaints of increased energy, psychomotor agitation or decreased need for sleep, and the lack of control of impulsivity is also usually greater in TB. Another important differential diagnosis is with substance intoxication or withdrawal, since TB often presents comorbidities with abuse or dependence on alcohol or other substances. Often, differential diagnosis is only possible through a toxicological survey of blood or urine.

TB is a psychopathological condition that presents one of the most delayed diagnoses. In general, the patient went through more than three doctors and received at least three incorrect diagnoses before being properly diagnosed. Psychopathologies that tend to increase impulses in general (bulimia, TOC, kleptomania, etc.), related to substance use, Anxiety Disorder, Unipolar Depression, Psychoses, Attention Deficit / Hyperactivity Disorder, Borderline Personality Disorder, Disorder Conduct, among others, may occur in comorbidity with TB; contributing to the worsening of the manic or mixed symptomatology, or constitute only a mixed or manic state. The differential diagnosis can be aided by the presence of family history of TB or alcoholism, age of early onset, episodic evolution, concomitance with accelerated thinking and increased energy and activation, as well as mood and affective changes. (ALCANTARA et al., 2003)

Due to the ignorance of the high prevalence of bipolar disorder (TB I and II, Cyclothymia, Hypomania and TB without other specification), the respective depressions are usually confused with exclusively unipolar conditions. In addition, a series of preceptors of Bipolar Disorder in depressed individuals considered unipolar, based on the clinical-epidemiological and therapeutic knowledge accumulated over the last years were evidenced:

- Family history of Bipolar Disorder in first-degree relatives;

- Mania or hypomania induced by antidepressants;

- Recurrent or brief depressive episodes (mean 3 months);

- Depression with multiple comorbidities;

- Substance-related anxiety disorder;

- Personality, eating, impulse control disorder;

- Loss of antidepressant effects (acute but not sustained response);

- Lack of response to three or more antidepressant trials.

Ultimately, unipolar or more non-bipolar depressions represent more benign prognosis and evolution, with no psychotic symptoms, no chronicity, no multiple recurrences and comorbidities, and no therapeutic resistance or worsening response to antidepressants. initiate later in patients without a family history of mood disorder or alcoholism. (MORENO et al., 2005 apud BARLOW, 2008)

Specific Features

The daily clinical practice with patients with Bipolar Disorder of Humor (TBH) reveals that the cases of comorbidity are quite frequent. Several epidemiological studies, including the National Comorbidity Survey (NCS) (KESSLER et al., 1994 apud SANCHES, ASSUNCAO, HETEM, 2005) confirm this fact. Comorbidity rates among patients with TBH range from 30% to almost 100%, depending on the methodology and sample selected. The main comorbidities in patients with TBH are substance abuse and anxiety disorders. Eating disorders, personality disorders and, among other diseases, hypothyroidism, migraine and obesity are also common. The latter are more common in women than in men with TBH (ARNOLD, 2003 apud Ibidem)

The prevalence of TB occurs in an equal proportion for both genders. Differently from Unipolar Depression, in which its incidence is higher in females: 1.9% males and 3.2% females. Its manifestations arise most commonly in groups with oscillating ages in their twenties and thirties. Studies on genetic factors also reveal their high heritability: ten times higher among first-degree relatives, with an incidence of 67% among Monozygotic Twins and 27% for Dizygotic Twins (KONRADI et al., 2004 apud VIEIRA, 2006)

However, there is no consensus in the literature regarding the main comorbidities present in TB, surveys reveal: 74.9% of any Anxiety Disorder; 42.3% Substance Abuse and 70.1% Multimorbity. Meta-analyzes also found an average suicide rate in patients with TB of 15%, about thirty times greater than in the general population (MERINKANGAS, 2007 apud KAPCZINSK; QUEVEDO, 2009)

	Any bipolar disorder, %	Bipolar I disorder, %	Bipolar II disorder, %	Subthreshold bipolar disorder, %
Any anxiety disorder	74.9	86.7	89.2	63.1
Panic disorder	20.1	29.1	27.2	12.1
Post-traumatic stress disorder	24.2	30.9	34.3	16.5
Generalised anxiety disorder	29.6	38.7	37.0	22.3
Social phobia	37.8	51.6	54.6	24.1
Obsessive–compulsive disorder	13.6	25.3	20.8	4.3
Attention-deficit hyperactivity disorder	31.4	40.6	42.3	23.0
Oppositional defiant disorder	36.8	44.4	38.2	32.8
Conduct disorder	30.3	43.8	18.6	28.9
Alcohol dependence	23.2	38.0	19.0	18.9
Drug dependence	14.0	30.4	8.7	9.5
One comorbid diagnosis	12.7	8.1	7.0	17.1
Two comorbid diagnoses	9.4	3.4	2.9	14.7
Three or more comorbid diagnoses	70.1	86.2	85.8	56.7

Table 3. Lifetime comorbidity of bipolar disorder with others disorders.

Treatments

The treatment of the euthymic patient should always consider the possibility of the patient having episodes of mania and / or depression. Euthymia is usually defined as the remission of symptoms, however, ideally, it would be the period in which the patient would not only be symptom free but functionally reintegrated into his or her routine activities. The goal of treatment, therefore, is to keep the patient without symptoms. Thus, the primary goal of treatment is remission and not just clinical response (50% reduction in observed symptoms), which is commonly used as a measure of outcome in clinical trials.

The treatment of Bipolar Disorder is divided into three phases: acute, continuation and maintenance. The goals of treatment during the acute phase are: treating mania without causing depression and / or consistently improving depression without causing mania. The continuation phase seeks to stabilize the benefits, reduce side effects, treat up remission, reduce the possibility of relapse, and increase overall functioning. Finally, the goals of treatment in the maintenance phase are to prevent mania and / or depression and maximize functional recovery, that is, that the patient continues in remission. (GOODWIN, 2003 apud SOUZA, 2005)

There is also a need for maintenance treatment in Bipolar Disorder (BD) because the recurrence rate is estimated to be 60% to 80% after discontinuation of lithium or antipsychotic therapy, and 20% to 50% for some other type of treatment (YAZICI et al., 2004 apud Ibidem) for TB. In addition, a considerable proportion of patients with TB, even those intensively monitored and adequately treated in acute episodes, will have residual disease-related morbidities. As a result, long-term treatment goals include not only prevention of suicidal behavior and recurrence of depression or mania, but also improvement of subsyndromic symptoms, adherence to treatment, quality of life, cognition, and functional outcomes.

Psychotherapy & Mood Stabilizers

Although pharmacological treatment is essential for the treatment of Bipolar Disorder, only 40% of all patients adhering to the medications remain asymptomatic during the follow-up period, which has led to the development of associated psychotherapeutic interventions. In this context, Knapp and Isolan (2005) point out that Cognitive-Behavioral Therapy (CBT) is a brief, structured, problem-solving therapy that involves active collaboration between patient and therapist to achieve established goals. The objectives of CBT in Bipolar Disorder are:

1. Educate patients and family members about Bipolar Disorder, its treatment and its difficulties associated with the disease;

2. Teach methods to monitor the occurrence, severity and course of symptoms;

3. Facilitating acceptance and cooperation in treatment;

4. Offer non-pharmacological techniques to deal with symptoms and problems;

5. To help the patient to face stressful factors that are interfering in the treatment;

6. Stimulating acceptance of the disease;

7. Increase the protective effect of the family;

8. Reduce the trauma and stigma associated with the disease.

Cognitive-Behavioral Therapy (CBT) has been the most widely studied psychotherapeutic approach in Bipolar Disorder. Several studies have demonstrated the efficacy of this technique in the treatment of patients with Bipolar Disorder, including those mentioned below. The first controlled study evaluating CBD in Bipolar Disorder was conducted by Cochran (1984), in which 28 bipolar patients were evaluated, comparing individual CBT with the usual treatment. Cochran used an approach that basically aimed to change cognitions and behaviors that interfered in drug adherence.

Patients who received CBT had higher adherence rates and lower rates of hospitalization at the end of the six-week treatment and after a six-month follow-up. Zaretsky et al. (1999) compared the effect of 20 sessions of CBT adapted for bipolar depression in 11 patients with bipolar depression using mood stabilizers with 11 controls with major depressive disorder receiving standard CBT. There was a significant decrease in depressive symptoms in both groups. Fava et al. (2001) evaluated CBT in 15 patients who relapsed despite using medication. The treatment consisted of ten 30-minute sessions each week, which focused on the treatment of residual symptoms and included psychoeducation, cognitive restructuring to expository therapy for depressive, anxious, and irritable symptoms. This treatment proved to be effective in the treatment of residual symptoms and increased the remission time of the disease. (KNAPP and ISOLAN, 2005)

Lam et al. (2000) performed one of the first controlled studies evaluating CBT in 25 patients with Bipolar Disorder. In this pilot study, CBT showed a significant decrease in bipolar episodes over a 12-month period compared to usual treatment. A recent clinical trial by Lam et al. (2003) analyzed 103 patients with Type I Bipolar Disorder who had frequent relapses despite adequate pharmacotherapy randomized to CBT or for usual treatment.

The cognitive-behavioral treatment consisted of 14 sessions in the first six months and two additional sessions in the following six months. In a 12-month follow-up period, patients who performed CBT had significantly fewer episodes of mood, fewer days in a bipolar mood episode, fewer hospitalizations, fewer subsyndromic symptoms, better coped with manic prodromes, and had better social functioning. After 2 years of the same clinical trial (Lam et al., 2005), no significant effect on relapse reduction was found, although the group receiving cognitive therapy again showed a significant reduction in the number of days of bipolar mood episodes, with significant improvement in mood scales, social functioning, strategies for coping with the prodromes of depression and mania, and dysfunctional interpersonal attitudes. (KNAPP and ISOLAN, 2005)

The evolution of TB is more complex due to the variability of clinical forms. It was agreed to measure the length of each episode by counting the elapsed time between the beginning and the end of each phase. In studies dating to the period before the onset of psychoactive drugs, the episodes lasted 4 to 13 months, the asymptomatic intervals became shorter, and the longer episodes even stabilized after the fourth or fifth episode (SELLARO, 2000 apud BARLOW, 2008).

Medications are crucial in treating Bipolar Disorder to decrease the intensity and number of episodes of the disorder. The need for such therapy may be justified by the strong genetic and biological burden of the disease. After all, genes and brain lesions can not be cured, but it is possible to control dysfunctions. The correct use of stabilizers such as lithium carbonate, for example, tends to decrease mortality (by suicide, accidents and diseases due to immune disorders of the body) up to seven times in bipolar patients. Mood stabilizers should be introduced early in treatment and be present for much of the time and can only be changed or withdrawn if there are clearly significant impairments related to them.

Medication should also be prescribed to lessen the instability of psychic and bodily functions - such as sleep and appetite. This basic therapy needs to be evaluated as a long-term strategy, since its results appear more clearly in months or even years. During the acute phases, antidepressants, or antipsychotics and benzodiazepines are often used in the manic and mixed phases. But pharmacology has limitations. Even residual symptoms, between stages, are not always amenable to total control. In addition, it is part of the clinical picture of the patient not to believe that they have any problem. Precisely for this reason, psychotherapy, although by itself is not enough, plays a fundamental role in helping the person to know better, to be more attentive to themselves, learning to recognize the symptoms. An important function of the therapy is to favor the commitment of the patient to the pharmacological treatment, since one of the main causes of crises is the abandonment of treatment.

In the acute phases of the disease, however, the role of the psychologist is supportive, it is restricted to support, with pain relief techniques that facilitate adherence to drug treatment, leaving behind the need to seek or discuss psychic senses for crises , since the intense symptoms of the patient make the therapeutic process more unproductive. After the acute phase, a period of rehabilitation is necessary, focusing on "psychoeducation".

At that moment, psychological counseling is usually decisive in a task as difficult as it is necessary: the reconstruction of the personal life after an affective episode, since after a serious occurrence of the disease it is common for the person to feel emotionally much affected. By improving it, it can be seen that professional and social life may have been seriously shaken and relationships with spouses, children, friends and family of origin deteriorated. In more severe cases, it is necessary to have the assistance of a therapeutic companion or an occupational therapist who helps the person to recover simple skills, such as bathing alone or going to the bank to withdraw money.

First Choice Maintenance

1. **LITHIUM**: There is good evidence that lithium is the main monotherapy in the treatment of TB. A meta-analysis of studies conducted before 1990 suggests that the magnitude of the prophylactic effect of lithium is greater for prevention of manic episodes than depressive episodes. This has been confirmed in recent clinical trials, which have shown clear benefit in preventing mania, but not in depression. Lithium also has anti-suicide properties. Rapid withdrawal of lithium therapy is associated with high rates of relapse in bipolar patients, even after good response and a good episode-free period. If lithium is discontinued, this should be done gradually. (GOODWIN & JAMISON, 1990 apud GORENSTEIN, 1999)

2. **LAMOTRIGINE**: Clinical trials have demonstrated the efficacy of Lamotrigine for prevention of relapse of TB in patients with a more recent manic episode, depressive, or fast cyclers. Lamotrigine has superior efficacy to placebo in prolonged use for manic episodes. This drug should not be used as monotherapy for bipolar patients if the prevention of relapse of mania is the major goal. Lamotrigine appears to have benefits for patients with type 2 TB with rapid cycling, and in some cases, monotherapy with Lamotrigine is adequate.

3. **VALPHORIC ACID**: Although a randomized clinical trial has not shown that Valproic Acid is superior to placebo in preventing relapse of bipolar episodes, in others it has been as effective as either Lithium or Olanzapine in preventing new episodes. In this negative

clinical trial, neither lithium nor Valproic Acid showed superiority in the primary measure of efficacy. However, a subanalysis showed that Valproic Acid was superior to placebo in severely ill patients. As the blinded studies and an open-label controlled trial showed equivalence of Valproic Acid and compared active drugs together with the great experience and excellent tolerability of this medication, Valproic Acid should be considered as the first line of treatment. (KUKOPULOS et al., 1980 apud Ibidem)

4. OLANZAPINE: Treatment with Olanzapine significantly reduces the rates of relapse of depressive and manic episodes compared to placebo and is as effective as Valproic Acid and Lithium in prolonging remission.

Drug	Depression	Mania	Prophylaxis	Relapse Prevention
Lithium	++	++	++++	++++
Valproate	+	+++	±	+
Carbamazepine	±	++	±	+
Lamotrigine	±	--	?	++
Olanzapine	--	+++	?	±
Aripiprazole	No data	++	?	±

Table 4. The number of replications and the consistency of the lithium literature set it apart from all other potential mood stabilizers in terms of evidence of prophylaxis. After lithium, similar kinds of evidence of likely benefit exist for lamotrigine, divalproex, and carbamazepine, with some differences (a single replication with lamotrigine, reliance on secondary analysis with divalproex, absence of placebo arms with carbamazepine). The antipsychotics do not truly assess or provide evidence of benefit in the maintenance phase of treatment, given the interpretation and rationale above. (GHAEMI, 2008)

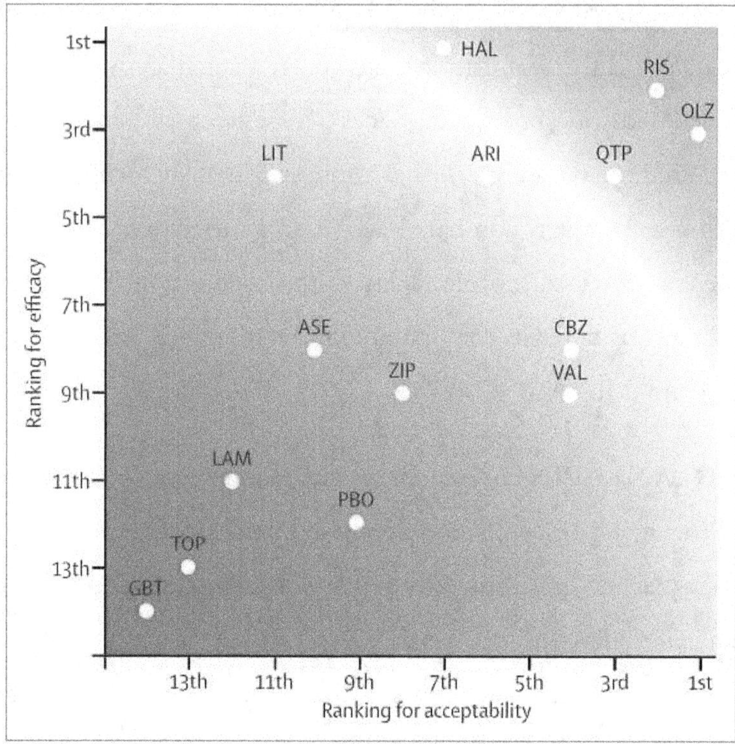

Figure 4. Ranking of antimanic drugs according to primary outcomes derived from multiple treatment meta-analysis. Efficacy is shown as a continuous outcome against the dropout rate. Treatments toward the red section combine the worst efficacy and tolerability profiles and treatments towards the green section combine the best profiles. ARI=aripiprazole. ASE=asenapine. CBZ=carbamazepine. VAL=valproate. GBT=gabapentin. HAL=haloperidol. LAM=lamotrigine. LIT=lithium. OLZ=olanzapine. PBO=placebo. QTP=quetiapine. RIS=risperidone. TOP=topiramate. ZIP=ziprasidone. (COUSINS DA, 2009 apud DELGADO; KAPCZINSKI; CHAVES, 2012)

Second Choice Maintenance

2.1. CARBAMAZEPINE: There are no large-scale studies, double-blind and placebo-controlled trials investigating the efficacy of Carbamazepine in the treatment of TB maintenance. However, most studies, but not all, have shown that Carbamazepine has better efficacy than Lithium and may have a better prophylactic efficacy than lithium in patients with non-classical mania presentations (eg incongruent mood pictures , type II TB comorbidities).

2.2. OTHER ATYPICAL ANTIPSYCHOTICS: Aripiprazole significantly prolongs the time to recurrence and significantly reduces the number of mood episodes compared to placebo in a 6-month clinical trial. However, a subanalysis showed that Aripiprazole was superior to placebo in preventing mania, but not in depression. Therefore, to date, this drug is recommended as a second-line treatment for bipolar patients with predominantly manic episodes. (KLEINDIENST et al., 2000 apud MACHADO-VIEIRA, 2003)

There are no double-blind clinical trials examining the long-term efficacy of Risperidone, Quetiapine or Ziprasidone for TB. Data from open studies suggest that risperidone may be effective in sustained TB improvement when used in combination with Lithium, Valproic Acid or Topiramate. Quetiapine alone or with mood stabilizers and monotherapy with Ziprasidone have also shown long-term improvements in open-label studies. (MACHADO-VIEIRA, 2003)

Third-Party Maintenance

3.1. CLOZAPINE: Combination therapy with Clozapine was significantly better than the usual treatment in a small, randomized, 6-month clinical trial. Evidence from the schizophrenia literature shows that Clozapine has anti-suicidal properties, suggesting the role of this agent in some TB patients.

3.2. ECT: Evidence from a series of cases suggests that maintenance ECT (commonly used together with medication) is effective in reducing hospitalizations in TB. However, a review concluded that ECT has an acute, but not a long-term, beneficial effect on suicidal ideation / behavior in patients with mood disorders (SHARMA et al., 2001 apud Ibidem)

Non-Recommended Maintenance

BENZODIAZEPINES: A systematic evaluation of benzodiazepines as prophylactic agents in TB has never been conducted, but factors such as dependence, rebound anxiety, memory impairment and discontinuation syndrome speak against its long-term use. Therefore, the absence of prophylactic efficacy and the risks associated with long-term use do not indicate this medication in the maintenance treatment of TB.

Combined Therapy

Combination therapy is an important option for patients who have not responded to treatment with a first-line monotherapy. However, there are no systematic comparisons of monotherapy against the use of combination treatments, and there is little evidence to recommend one combination over the other. Combinations that have shown effectiveness include: Lithium + Valproic Acid or Carbamazepine; as well as Lithium or Valproic Acid + Olanzapine or Risperidone. No data are available on Lithium + Lamotrigine, but this combination is recommended based on its confirmed prophylactic effects as monotherapy. (TONDO et al., 1997 apud SOUZA, 2005)

Monotherapy With Antidepressants

Although antidepressants have efficacy in acute depressive episodes, a review with 7 randomized trials of antidepressants (predominantly tricyclics) as monotherapy or in combination therapy concludes that they are not effective in preventing future episodes. In a 1973 maintenance study, manic episodes occurred in 12% of patients using lithium, 33% in placebo patients, and 66% in patients using mood stabilizers with imipramine monotherapy had a manic-turn, compared to only 11% of those who were randomized to combination therapy with Bupropion (SACHS et al., 1994 apud CLEMENTE, 2015)

These data clearly suggest that tricyclics destabilize the course of TB when used as monotherapy with SSRIs for the treatment of TB maintenance. However, in a 1-year clinical trial comparing lithium, Valproic Acid and placebo, in which patients received SSRIs for depressive episodes, a significantly large proportion of patients discontinued the study in the SSRI + placebo group compared to the SSRI + Valproic acid. In addition, SSRI monotherapy is also not recommended for treatment of TB. (GYULAI et al., 2003 apud Ibidem)

Medications	Weight Gain	Metabolic Syndrome	Dyslipidemia	Neurological Effects	Dermatological Reactions
Lithium	++	+	+	-	-
Valproic Acid	+++	+	+	in pregnant	rash

Lamotrigine	-	-	-	-	rash, SSJ, Risk 14 x larger
Carbamazepine	-	-	-	-	rash, SSJ
Olanzapine	+++	++	OR 1.5	-	-
Quetiapine	++	++	OR 1.4	-	-
Risperidone	++	++	OR 1.5	SEP	-
Ziprasidone	-	-	-	SEP	-
Aripiprazole	-	-	-	-	-
Clozapine	+++	++	OR 1.8	-	-
A. Typical	+	+	OR 1.2	SEP	-

Table 5. Summary of Side Effects of Drugs Used in Treatment of TB Maintenance. +++ = high probability, - = small probability. SSJ = Stevens Jonhson syndrome. SEP = extrapyramidal syndrome. OR = probability that the event will occur if it is greater than. (KETTER, 2010 apud ABP, 2012)

Other Agents

Open studies and preliminary data suggest combined use with Oxcarbazepine or Phenytoin. Open studies also suggest efficacy of topiramate added to mood stabilizers, or atypical antipsychotics. Combination therapy with Gabapentin was effective for some patients who responded to this agent in the acute phase, but 30% of patients experienced loss of efficacy over time. In a 4-month clinical trial, omega-3 prolonged remission time compared to placebo. Flupentixol does not appear to have prophylactic efficacy in patients with TB. Agents such as gabapentin, topiramate and calcium channel blockers have been investigated for use in TB, but there are insufficient data recommending their use as monotherapy. (STOLL et al., 1999 apud MACHADO-VIEIRA, 2007)

The clinical use of cytokines and neuropeptides could also represent new potential targets for the development of novel pharmacological treatments for mood disorders. Recently, specific non-peptidergic galanin GAL3 receptor antagonists (SNAP-37889 and SNAP-398299) have shown anti-depressant properties but still need to be confirmed by controlled clinical studies. Although they lack replication in new controlled studies, phenytoin, oxcarbazepine, leviracetam, topiramate and high doses of thyroid potentiation may have therapeutic effects on TB (whether in mania, depression or maintenance therapy), and may also represent promising potentiation therapies for refractory TB. Other effective options for treatment-resistant cases include monoamine oxidase inhibitors 50 Somatic treatment may also play a role in the treatment of treatment-resistant depression, including vagus nerve stimulation (VNS), transcranial magnetic stimulation (TMS) , and deep brain stimulation (ECP). (OGREN, 2006 apud MACHADO-VIEIRA, 2007)

Similarly, bipolar depression therapy is a challenging and critical topic and has also been associated with high rates of treatment-resistant cases. The use of antidepressants in bipolar depression is not clearly established. The combination of antidepressant and mood stabilizers is widely used, but the appropriate dose and duration of treatment of the different agents have not been clearly defined. Although they demonstrate a considerable efficacy in bipolar depression, the antidepressants can cause the polarity change and abrupt mood alterations, increasing the risk of rapid cycling and refractory mood disorders.

In general, it has been proposed that antidepressants, lamotrigine or topiramate (combined with a mood stabilizer) are first-line treatments for bipolar 1 depression. For example, in a large, double-blind, controlled (n = 191) with placebo, lamotrigine showed superior antidepressant efficacy compared to placebo after seven days. Topiramate also had antidepressant efficacy in bipolar depression, rapid cycling, acute mania and mixed treatment resistant episodes. In addition, the use of a combination strategy with antidepressants and an atypical antipsychotic has been advocated, but there is a lack of convincing data demonstrating that the combination is more effective than the use of an antidepressant alone. (VIETA, 2002 apud SOUZA, 2005)

Many approaches have been proposed for treatment-resistant TB. It is surprising that only psychotherapies have been specifically validated in large-scale controlled clinical trials as adjunctive treatment to pharmacological agents. Over the last decade, specific psychotherapeutic approaches have been studied, including group psychoeducation, family focused treatment (TFF), cognitive therapy (TC), and interpersonal and social rhythm therapy (TIRS).

These approaches are jointly tested to validate their efficacy in a specific structure and proposed target outcomes, including a decrease in the number of episodes and subsyndromal symptoms, greater adherence to treatment, and improved social functioning. In acute mania, randomized, double-blind, placebo-controlled studies demonstrated that olanzapine and risperidone, in combination with lithium or valproate, induced a superior improvement compared to an isolated mood stabilizer. (MACHADO-VIEIRA, 2007)

About the Author

MARCUS DEMINCO (Salvador – BA, Brazil. Set, 28 1976) is a Brazilian writer and psychologist; Doctor Honoris Causa in Attention Deficit Disorder/ Hyperactivity (TDAH); *Practitioner* and Tutor of Neuro-linguistic programming (NLP), author of scientific articles for the Portal of Psychologists. Owner of several sentences, texts and thoughts shared on social networks and websites, and from the popular text "Why read Paulo Coelho?" - praised by the writer Paulo Coelho himself among his readers. In addition, Marcus Deminco is also the author of the books:

1. VERTYGO – The Suicide of Lukas.
2. The Secret of Clarice Lispector.
3. Me and My Friend ADD - Autobiography of a guy with Attention Deficit Disorder.
4. Messages to Post, Like and Share. Vol.1
5. Messages to Post, Like and Share. Vol.2

6. Messages to Post, Like and Share. Vol.3
7. Neuro-Linguistic Programming: beginning by the beginning.
8. E-cards text collection. Vol. 1
9. E-cards text collection. Vol.2

— Awards and Tributes—

1.1. Author of "Estafeta Sem Rumo" — Cecilio Barros Barros Pessoa Awards of Anthology — Academy of Letters, Arts and Sciences of Arraial do Cabo, RJ.

1.2. Doctor Honoris Causa in ADHD by the Brazilian Association of Psychosomatic Medicine in recognition of the scientific contribution and social relevance of the book: Me & My Friend ADHD − Autobiography of a guy with Attention Deficit Disorder.

1.3. One of the winners of Além da Terra, Além do Céu prize of contemporary poetry awarded by Chiado Editora (Portugal).

— Talk to Marcus Deminco—

E-mail: marcusdeminco@gmail.com
Website: http://marcusdeminco.com/
Blog: http://marcusdeminco.blogspot.com.br/
Twitter: https://twitter.com/marcusdeminco
Facebook: https://www.facebook.com/marcus.deminco
Pinterest: https://www.pinterest.com/marcusdeminco/
Instagram: @marcusdeminco
Youtube: https://www.youtube.com/channel/UCRu8yfSoLewjuX6GO6o7Nmw
G+: https://plus.google.com/u/0/114858320913983491464
Tumblr: http://deminco.tumblr.com/
Flickr: https://www.flickr.com/photos/143729713@N06/with/28004881736/
GoodReads: https://www.goodreads.com/author/show/7792932.Marcus_Deminco/
Pensador: https://pensador.uol.com.br/autor/marcus_deminco/

References

ALCANTARA, Igor et al . **Avanços no diagnóstico do transtorno do humor bipolar.** Rev. psiquiatr. Rio Gd. Sul, Porto Alegre , v. 25, supl. 1, p. 22-32, Apr. 2003. Available from   <http://www.scielo.br/scielo.php?script=sci_arttext&pid=S0101-81082003000400004&lng=en&nrm=iso>.   access on 31 Mar. 2018. http://dx.doi.org/10.1590/S0101-81082003000400004.

ALDA, Martin. **Transtorno Bipolar.** Rev. Bras. Psiquiatr., São Paulo , v. 21, supl. 2, p. 14-17,   Oct.   1999   .   Available   from <http://www.scielo.br/scielo.php?script=sci_arttext&pid=S1516-44461999000600005&lng=en&nrm=iso>.   access   on   03   Apr.   2018. http://dx.doi.org/10.1590/S1516-44461999000600005.

ANDREASEN, Nancy, C; BLACK, Donald W. **Introdução a psiquiatria.** Artmed: 2009

Associação   Brasileira   de   Transtorno   Bipolar.   Available   from: < http://www.abtb.org.br/transtorno.php >. Access on 03 Apr. 2018.

BALDAÇARA, Leonardo. **Transtornos Mentais.** Palmas, 2015.

BALLONE,   GJ.   **Estabilizadores   do   Humor.**   PsiqWeb.   Available   from: <www.psiqweb.med.br >. Access on 03 Apr. 2018.

BALONNE, GJ. **CID-10 - Classificação Estatística Internacional de Doenças e Problemas   Relacionados   com   a   Saúde.**   Psi.Web.   Available   from: < http://www.psicologia.com.pt/ >. Access on 03 Apr. 2018.

BALONNE, GJ. **DSM-V - Manual de Diagnóstico e Estatística das Perturbações Mentais.** Psi.Web. Available from: < http://www.psicologia.com.pt/ >. Access on 03 Apr. 2018.

BARLOW, David H. DURAND, V. Mark. **Psicopatologia: uma abordagem integrada.** 4ª Ed. Trad.: Roberto Galman. São-Paulo: Cengage Learning, 2008.

BOSAIPO NB, BORGES VF, JURUENA MF.**Transtorno Bipolar: uma revisão dos aspectos conceituais e clínicos. Medicina** (Ribeirão Preto, Online.) 2016;50(Supl.1),jan-fev.:72-84. Available from: < http://revista.fmrp.usp.br/2017/vol50-Supl-1/SIMP8-Transtorno-Bipolar.pdf>. Access on 03 Apr. 2018.

CLEMENTE, Adauto Silva. **Concepções dos psiquiatras sobre o Transtorno Bipolar do humor e sobre o estigma a ele associado**. Belo Horizonte: FIOCRUZ, 2015. Available from: <http://www.cpqrr.fiocruz.br/texto-completo/T_82.pdf >. Access on 03 Apr. 2018.

CHEN C- H, Suckling J, Lennox BR, Ooi C, Bullmore ET. **A quantitative meta- analysis of fMRI studies in bipolar disorder**. Bipolar Disord 2011: 13: 1–15. The Authors Journal compilation 2011 John Wiley & Sons A/S. Available from: <http://news.wiley.com/WorldBipolarDay?elq_mid=25920&elq_cid=5875954>. Access on 03 Apr. 2018.

DEL PORTO, José Alberto. **Conceito e diagnóstico**. Rev. Bras. Psiquiatr. São Paulo, v. 21, supl. 1, p. 06-11, May 1999. Available from <http://www.scielo.br/scielo.php?script=sci_arttext&pid=S1516-44461999000500003&lng=en&nrm=iso>. access on 31 Mar. 2018. http://dx.doi.org/10.1590/S1516-44461999000500003.

DELGADO, V.B.; KAPCZINSKI, F.; CHAVES, M.L.F.. **Memory mood congruency phenomenon in bipolar I disorder and major depression disorder patients**. Braz J Med Biol Res, Ribeirão Preto , v. 45, n. 9, p. 856-861, Sept. 2012 . Available from <http://www.scielo.br/scielo.php?script=sci_arttext&pid=S0100-879X2012000900010&lng=en&nrm=iso>. access on 22 Apr. 2018. Epub June 21, 2012 http://dx.doi.org/10.1590/S0100-879X2012007500098.

DELGALARRONDO, Paulo. **Psicopatologia e semiologia dos transtornos mentais**. Porto Alegre: ArtMed, 2000.

DEL-PORTO, José Alberto; DEL-PORTO, Kátia Oddone. **História da caracterização nosológica do Transtorno Bipolar**. Rev. psiquiatr. clín., São Paulo , v. 32, supl. 1, p. 7-14, 2005 . Available from <http://www.scielo.br/scielo.php?script=sci_arttext&pid=S0101-60832005000700002&lng=en&nrm=iso>. access on 31 Mar. 2018. http://dx.doi.org/10.1590/S0101-60832005000700002.

Dicionário de Especialidades Farmacêuticas. São Paulo: JBM Farma, 2005.

FLECK, Marcelo P. et al . **Revisão das diretrizes da Associação Médica Brasileira para o tratamento da depressão (Versão integral)**. Rev. Bras. Psiquiatr., São Paulo , v. 31, supl. 1, p. S7-S17, May 2009 . Available from <http://www.scielo.br/scielo.php?script=sci_arttext&pid=S1516-44462009000500003&lng=en&nrm=iso>. access on 03 Apr. 2018. http://dx.doi.org/10.1590/S1516-44462009000500003.

FRANGOU, S. **Uma perspectiva neurocientífica de sistemas de esquizofrenia e transtorno bipolar**. Schizophrenia Bulletin, Volume 40, Issue 3, 1 May 2014, Pages 523–531. Available

from:<https://academic.oup.com/schizophreniabulletin/article/40/3/523/1906284>
Access on 03 Apr. 2018.

GHAEMI, Nassir S. **Toward a Hippocratic psychopharmacology**. Canadian journal of psychiatry. Revue canadienne de psychiatrie 53(3):189-96. April 2008. DOI: 10.1177/070674370805300309.

GORENSTEIN, Clarice; SCAVONE, Cristóforo. **Avanços em psicofarmacologia - mecanismos de ação de psicofármacos hoje.** Revista Brasileira de Psiquiatria. Available from: < http://www.scielo.br/pdf/rbp/v21n1/v21n1a11.pdf >. Access on 03 Apr. 2018.

KAPCZINSKI, Flávio. **Tratamento Farmacológico do Transtorno Bipolar.** Porto Alegre: Revista de Psiquiatria Clínica. Available from:< http://www.hcnet.usp.br/ipq/revista/vol32/s1/34.html >. Access on 03 Apr. 2018.

KAPCZINSKI, Flávio; QUEVEDO, João et al. **Transtorno Bipolar: Teoria e Clínica**. Porto Alegre: Artmed, 2009.

KNAPP, P.; ISOLAN, L. **Abordagens psicoterápicas no Transtorno Bipolar**. Rev. Psiq. Clín. 32, supl 1; 98-104, 2005. Available from:< http://www.scielo.br/pdf/rpc/v32s1/24418.pdf>. Access on 03 Apr. 2018.

LAMBERT, Kelly. KINSLEY, Craig H. **Neurociência Clínica: as bases neurobiológicas da saúde**. Trad.: Ronaldo Cataldo. Porto Alegre: Artmed, 2006.

LIMA, I.V.M.; Sougey, E.B.; Vallada Filho, H.P. **Genética dos transtornos afetivos.** São Paulo: Rev. Psiq. Clín., 2004.

LOUZÃ e ELKIS. **Psiquiatria Básica.** Artmed, 2007

MACHADO-VIEIRA, Rodrigo; SOARES, Jair C. **Transtornos de humor refratários a tratamento.** Rev. Bras. Psiquiatr., São Paulo , v. 29, supl. 2, p. S48-S54, Oct. 2007 . Available from <http://www.scielo.br/scielo.php?script=sci_arttext&pid=S1516-44462007000600003&lng=en&nrm=iso>. access on 03 Apr. 2018. Epub Aug 13, 2007. http://dx.doi.org/10.1590/S1516-44462006005000058.

MACHADO-VIEIRA, Rodrigo et al . **Neurobiologia do transtorno de humor bipolar e tomada de decisão na abordagem psicofarmacológica.** Rev. psiquiatr. Rio Gd. Sul, Porto Alegre , v. 25, supl. 1, p. 88-105, abr. 2003. Available from: <http://www.scielo.br/scielo.php?script=sci_arttext&pid=S0101-81082003000400010&lng=pt&nrm=iso>. Access on 03 Apr. 2018.

Manual Diagnóstico e Estatístico de Transtornos Mentais, 5° ed. (APA, 2018)

MEDPLAN. **O tratamento farmacológico do Transtorno Bipolar na infância e na adolescência.** Available from: < http://www.medplan.com.br/materias >. Access on 03 Apr. 2018.

MORENO, D.H.; MORENO, R.A. Rev. Psiq. Clín. 32, supl 1; 56-62, 2005. **Estados mistos e quadros de ciclagem rápida no Transtorno Bipolar.** Available from:<http://www.scielo.br/pdf/rpc/v32s1/24413.pdf>. Access on 03 Apr. 2018.

MORENO, Ricardo. **Novos anticonvulsivantes no tratamento do transtorno do humor bipolar: manejo clínico, eficácia e tolerância.** São Paulo: Revista de Psiquiatria clínica. Available from: < http://www.hcnet.usp.br/ipq/revista/vol26/n6/art288.html>. Access on 03 Apr. 2018.

MORENO, Ricardo Alberto; MORENO, Doris Hupfeld; RATZKE, Roberto. **Diagnóstico, tratamento e prevenção da mania e da hipomania no Transtorno Bipolar.** Rev. psiquiatr. clín., São Paulo , v. 32, supl. 1, p. 39-48, 2005 . Available from <http://www.scielo.br/scielo.php?script=sci_arttext&pid=S0101-60832005000700007&lng=en&nrm=iso>. Access on 03 Apr. 2018. http://dx.doi.org/10.1590/S0101-60832005000700007.

MOTTA, Paulo. **Genética Humana: Aplicada a Psicologia e Toda a Área Biomédica.** Rio de Janeiro: Guanabara Koogan, 2005.

NETO, M. R. Louzã; ELKIS, Hélio. **Psiquiatria Básica.** Porto Alegre: Artmed, 2009.

OPAS (Organização Pan-Americana da Saúde). Available from: < http://www.opas.org.br/opas.cfm >. Access on 03 Apr. 2018.

RIBEIRO, Marcelo; LARANJEIRA, Ronaldo; CIVIDANES, Giuliana. **Transtorno Bipolar do humor e uso indevido de substâncias psicoativas.** Rev. psiquiatr. clín. São Paulo , v. 32, supl. 1, p. 78-88, 2005 . Available from <http://www.scielo.br/scielo.php?script=sci_arttext&pid=S0101-60832005000700012&lng=en&nrm=iso>. access on 31 Mar. 2018. http://dx.doi.org/10.1590/S0101-60832005000700012.

SANCHES, Rafael F.; ASSUNCAO, Sheila; HETEM, Luiz Alberto B. **Impacto da comorbidade no diagnóstico e tratamento do Transtorno Bipolar.** Rev. psiquiatr. clín. São Paulo , v. 32, supl. 1, p. 71-77, 2005 . Available from <http://www.scielo.br/scielo.php?script=sci_arttext&pid=S0101-60832005000700011&lng=en&nrm=iso>. access on 31 Mar. 2018. http://dx.doi.org/10.1590/S0101-60832005000700011.

SOUZA, F.G.M. **Tratamento do Transtorno Bipolar – Eutimia.** Rev. Psiq. Clín. 32, supl 1; 63-70, 2005. Available from:< http://www.scielo.br/pdf/rpc/v32s1/24414.pdf>. Access on 03 Apr. 2018.

SZMULEWICZ, Alejandro G. et al . **An updated review on the neuropsychological profile of subjects with bipolar disorder**. Arch. Clin. Psychiatry, São Paulo , v. 42, n. 5, p. 139-146, Oct. 2015 . Available from <http://www.scielo.br/scielo.php?script=sci_arttext&pid=S0101-60832015000500139&lng=en&nrm=iso>. access on 22 Apr. 2018. http://dx.doi.org/10.1590/0101-60830000000064.

TENG, Chei Tung; CEZAR, Luiz Teixeira Sperry. **Como Diagnosticar e Tratar Depressão** 2010. Available from: <http://www.moreirajr.com.br/revistas.asp?fase=r003&id_materia=4526 >. Access on 03 Apr. 2018.

TUNG, T.C. **Enigma Bipolar- Conseqüências, Diagnóstico E Tratamento Do Transtorno Bipolar.** São Paulo: MG Editores, 2007.

VIEIRA, Rodrigo. **As bases neurobiológicas do Transtorno Bipolar.** Porto Alegre: Revista de Psiquiatria Clínica. Available from: <http://www.hcnet.usp.br/ipq/revista/vol32/s1/28.html>. Access on 03 Apr. 2018.

ZUNG S, MICHELON L, CORDEIRO Q. **O uso do lítio no Transtorno Afetivo Bipolar.** Arq Med Hosp Fac Cienc Med Santa Casa São Paulo. 2010; 55(1):30-7. Available from: <http://www.fcmsantacasasp.edu.br/images/Arquivos_medicos/2010/55_1/08_AR3.pdf. >. Access on 03 Apr. 2018.

www.ingramcontent.com/pod-product-compliance
Lightning Source LLC
Chambersburg PA
CBHW061504250726
48657CB00005B/1716